From Coconut Trees To Cults

Mike Davis

Published by Mike Davis, 2024.

While every precaution has been taken in the preparation of this book, the publisher assumes no responsibility for errors or omissions, or for damages resulting from the use of the information contained herein.

FROM COCONUT TREES TO CULTS

First edition. August 13, 2024.

Copyright © 2024 Mike Davis.

ISBN: 979-8227998828

Written by Mike Davis.

Background and Introduction

Hi, and thanks for reading my book on the evolution of religion.

Religion has evolved because our human ancestors likely had no religion when they emerged from the sea and for a very long time after that—it was developed over time.

I'm offering this book in both audiobook and e-book formats. If you have the e-book and read a statement saying "listening," you are reading the text; I missed that when I edited the audio to electronic format.

I also found some words as I built my audiobook like read, as in "I read this book," that should sound red (as in the past participle), were mispronounced by my AI buddy. In those cases, I have changed the spelling to "r-e-d" in the example I'm using so that it sounds correct. I will try to fix those few instances for the e-book, but if you are reading the e-book and come across what looks like a typo, that is likely the case.

A little bit about myself: I live in Seattle with my wife, Gale. We're animal lovers (though currently furry-less) and politically progressive. We love music, food, wine, live theater, and good books. Writing has been a long-time passion of mine. I have several self-published books, including the original version of this essay, which is now this audiobook format. I plan to convert some of my other works to audio to broaden my potential audience.

Furthermore, I maintain a website, irishmikedavis.com, where I post articles and showcase my books. You can also find me on Facebook under the Irish Mike Davis handle. Be forewarned: I'm a proud liberal, as most of my blog posts will demonstrate, but humor is also a mainstay on my site.

Alright, that's enough about me. Let's delve into our story about religion!

Prologue

The title of this book, *From Coconut Trees To Religious Cults*, references the evolutionary journey from when our ancestors climbed down from the trees to where we are today, including a few extreme examples of devotion bordering on cultism.

Everything in the known universe is in motion and changing. Our galaxy, solar system, and planet are in constant motion. Everything is evolving. Stars are exploding and imploding like popcorn kernels in a giant pot of boiling oil. Planets and galaxies disintegrate. The debris from these massive detonations coalesces into new planets. Solar systems and galaxies devour each other like a hotdog-eating contest at the state fair. And human spirituality is changing and evolving.

In the beginning, some four and a half billion years ago, according to current science, our earth was a cauldron of liquefied rock, boiling oceans. There must have been devastating earthquakes. Immense atmospheric events of unimaginable proportions rendered life as we know it today almost impossible.

In spite of the continuing earthquakes that today nudge the Earth's continental plates one way or another, mighty volcanoes spewing layers of flowing lava and ash to blanket the Earth and create new land masses, typhoons, monsoons, tornadoes, and tsunamis, our Earth is quiet compared to its fiery beginnings.

All this activity is the essence of evolution. Everything in our universe is in motion and changing, including planets, galaxies, and atoms. So are human notions about faith and a supreme deity.

Theories and beliefs about religions bump into each other, setting off a chain reaction of examination and debates. Whether you believe that a god, any god, or many gods are responsible for the creation of us and our universe or not, it seems evident that the first edition of God's work was far from perfect. What might someday be the finished product will most likely be the return of our planet to the cosmic dust from whence we came.

Will another planet in our universe support life as we know it, and will our history begin all over again? That may have already happened somewhere in our vast universe. Scientists tell us our sun and planet will die. Whatever may happen to us is still billions of years into the future, but the end will come.

Like our universe and our world, religion has evolved and is still evolving. Like our earth and the universe, religious evolution has often been quite violent. The evolution of religion and imagination is fascinating and bewildering. I will share with you some of that history and my thoughts on the topic.

Warning! If you are devoutly religious, or even casually devout, and the questioning of the various teachings of faith or the idea of challenging the existence of God makes you go into an uncontrollable rage in search of high-powered automatic weapons, read no further.

It may seem to some that I am attacking religion. I am honestly not. What I am doing and have spent a significant portion of my life of eighty-two years doing is trying to understand the grip religion has on so many people.

Why does religion seem to mesmerize some and repulse others? Why do we seem to need religion to cope with the everyday ups and downs of life, birth, death, disaster, and winning Super Bowls? We have all heard athletes proclaim, "I want to thank Jesus Christ for leading us to victory." I have never heard a loser blame Jesus Christ or God for the loss. Can it be that God, if such an entity exists, is interested in a damn football game?

While I may well be critical of religion, my disdain is aimed more at the people who perverted religion for their selfish gains.

Most religions are not the problem, but rather the people who twist their philosophy to fit their political, psychological, or material needs. That includes Christians, Muslims, Jews, Buddhists, or anyone with any other spiritual pursuit.

With some exceptions, the Old Testament of Christianity is born of the Jewish Torah, as is the Quran, and they seem to focus on vengeance and reprisal for the imperfection of humans.

Meanwhile, the New Testament, claiming to contain Jesus's words, emphasizes love and tolerance over hatred and intolerance. Having cited both the Torah and the Quran, I must admit that I have never read either text in its entirety; I have read a fair number of excerpts. Some may claim that what I say in this book qualifies as a type of religion since I am espousing what I believe has led to the state of modern-day religions.

One definition of religion in Webster is "an interest, a belief, or an activity that is very important to a person or group." I have both an interest and a belief that is very important to me: atheism. Any philosophy that informs your thoughts, behavior, and beliefs is, thus, a religion. So, I agree with that contention.

To the best of our knowledge, the rest of the animal kingdom has no concept of religion. They accept their fate in life without a higher power orchestrating their lives or their deaths. There is no evidence that they have a sense of the passage of time, save reacting to daylight and darkness by sleeping, awakening, and following other instinctive routines.

The cow might think the grass is greener on the other side of the fence, but they seem content to spend their day grazing in fields of grass, pooping mindlessly, and heading back to the barn for milking.

However, animals have a sense of life or a value of life. Why else would the antelope run like hell when one of the large cats is in the neighborhood rather than lay down and become a meal? Every animal that is a tasty treat for a predator seems to be very aware of the danger of losing its life. But do they consider the prospect of an afterlife? There's no sign of this, and I doubt that they do. Still, life or the preservation of their life seems paramount.

If you are as fascinated as I am by mankind's journey on this earth, our evolving humanity, our inhumanity, our progress, our stumbles, and sociology, which has to include the story of religion and its central role in human development, then you might enjoy listening further. You may not agree with all my assumptions or conclusions, but hopefully, you will ponder some of what I have to say.

My hope in offering this audiobook is to engage minds in a philosophical, social, and historical examination of the evolution of religion. A narrative of the origins and effects of religion on the human experience. Some listeners might work to improve religion, and others may, like me, move away from faith.

I don't know if this audiobook is a narrative history, historical fiction, or a combination of both. I have done a good deal of reading and research, which might suggest that it is a narrative-historical approach. Yet, this is also full of my opinions, theories, and conclusions, many of which will be accepted by some and rejected by others. In some cases, there is little or no evidence to support my thesis, making it empirically based and, thus, historical fiction. I am okay with that.

I learned long ago that my role in life is to explore ideas and present them to others for consideration. While some may label me a lunatic or misguided, my intent is to engage others' minds and start them thinking and talking. From that, I hope we evolve a better understanding of each other and the world in which we live. A more peaceful world would be a wonderful thing.

Though not a sociologist by education or trade, I find that I've spent my life fascinated by who and what we are as a species. Being Irish, I suspect I have a genetic predisposition for that sort of thing, and since I'm a terrible poet, I resort to espousing my thoughts in a tutorial or lecture form.

Over history, many people more intelligent than I have pondered the enigma of religion, but few of them have been more consumed with the topic than I have been throughout my life. I'm not sure why I find it so fascinating; it is just who I am.

If I could begin again, knowing what I think I know now, which is not only impossible but may suggest I hold an inflated view of my knowledge, I might have pursued some form of sociology as my chosen career instead of an engineer, but alas, it is far too late for that.

As I examine the topic of religion, I intend to employ a technique taken from journalism known as the 5 W's: Who? What? When? Where? & Why? Not necessarily in that order. There is a sort of sixth W, but the letter is at the end of the word, and that word is "How." I may revisit one or more of those questions at times as I work my way through this mind-bending topic, and at other times, I may discuss more than one W within a chapter or section. You, dear listener, will have to deal with the vagaries of my mind. As humans, we seldom segregate into cleanly defined categories, and that necessitates the overlapping of the notions of who we are.

Founded on my own life experiences, this narrative is based on a fair amount of reading and study and a lifetime of observation, thought, and examining not only the beliefs and behavior of others but also my own beliefs and actions, which, while not always noble, have evolved. Where I am able to draw from the wealth of knowledge developed over several thousands of years, I plan to do just that.

Anything I believe to be an original thought when, in fact, someone else has made the same point renders my failure to attribute to that source accidental, incidental, or coincidental. The truth is, few of us have original thoughts anymore. New ideas and philosophies are few and far between after all the millennia of human inquisition.

While something I have considered, discussed, thought about, conjured up, or read over my many years might feel like a revelation to me, it is likely that someone, somewhere, has had the same idea or thought or something quite close to it.

If I have not encountered their words or thoughts or hit on them through some mental osmosis and concluded the statements were my creation and fail to attribute the words to the original author, it is an honest mistake and not an effort to plagiarize the work of others.

These last couple of statements are intended to keep the lawyers at bay or, at a minimum, provide a defense against charges of plagiarism by an overzealous lawyer facing large car payments.

Before moving on, I would like to dedicate this book to some of the people who have played essential roles in my life and still do, and some who, because they existed, I now exist. My parents are the first of those in the existence column of attributes.

My father, Clarence Edward Davis, whom I never knew and who is but a faint memory from one meeting on my fourth birthday, most certainly bears some responsibility for who I am on a genetic level. My mother, Goldie Cecelia Connolly, whom I knew for only a short time from my teen years to my early twenties before she died, is also a player. It is from her that I inherited my Irish tendencies to talk too much. So, she and my father are contributors by passing on their genes.

My parents and family played no role in shaping who I am through the nurturing process. I assume that my passion for philosophy, curiosity, and passion for examining life must come from my genetic makeup.

I want to dedicate this to my wife, Gale, who, like me, has a passion for life, a need to find answers, and strong opinions on a wide range of topics. Putting up with my nonsense and unhinged sense of humor has required the spirit and endurance of a Joan of Arc. As I record this, we are approaching our fiftieth wedding anniversary, a feat neither of us ever dreamed possible when we first met.

Over the years, we have spent countless hours in deep and sometimes heated debate, most often with a glass of wine in hand, discussing all things related to the human condition. Gale has had to suffer hours of my pontification on one topic or another, and for that, among many other reasons, I love her more than I can express.

I often joke that I pull this train of soapboxes behind me as I travel through life, something like a toddler with a rope full of quacking wooden ducks. Given the opportunity, I will mount one of those soapboxes and begin quacking philosophically about the meaning of life.

Gale's intellect and willingness to challenge my conclusions have prevented me from closing my mind to new and different ideas or charging over a cliff of ignorance. Her steadfast love and patience have provided an invaluable grounding and kept me from doing more stupid things than I have done. She is my touchstone to reality.

And last but certainly not least, to my children, Tracy, Joey, and Sean. If they do not always agree with my conclusions or theories, they have a good deal of my curiosity and a penchant for questioning the status quo. Their love and support, in spite of my sporadic involvement in their formative years, is one of my true treasures. The life of an absent father is a complicated and emotionally draining one. I'm not asking for pity; I'm making an observation.

My Story

It seems logical to discuss my life's journey next, which will lead us to where I reside philosophically today.

While my story is relatively atypical—and it seems to me primarily dull—and I suspect most people think their personal story is boring, I believe it is relevant to who I am today, as are the formative years of most children.

I like to characterize small children as being like baby ducks who have lost their mother; they will attach themselves to any entity that comes along and appears to them to be a person or animal of authority and protection and follow those elders everywhere they go, even if that means the end of the earth. They understand instinctively that they are babies, and their survival depends on attaching themselves to another living being with the hope their chosen mentor can guide them through the gauntlet of life. If they pick wisely, they should do well; if not...well.

My purpose in sharing my particular story here is not to enlist any sympathy for my somewhat different childhood, but to provide a context or background for what I will share with listeners during this conversation about religion; it is relevant. I also prefer to think that I am still learning today at the somewhat advanced age of eighty-two, and some of these views, albeit a minority, could change in the future.

I was born curious, as I mentioned in acknowledging my parents. I have always sought answers to things I didn't understand. I have always looked for ways to improve virtually anything with which I came into contact, and I do not readily accept the status quo or statements like, "That is just the way it has always been." That statement will typically become a personal challenge for me to prove otherwise.

A case in point about my curiosity concerns an incident involving my grandfather when I was about four years old. He wasn't my grandfather by blood but rather my grandmother's cohabitating boyfriend, friend, or border. I never knew for sure which label was appropriate.

Information garnered later in life intimated that he may have been the father of an illegitimate child born to my grandmother long before I was born. This event likely led to her separation from my biological grandfather, whom I met once. It almost certainly produced a spate of gossip. Since no one can validate this, it lives on as a legend, as does much that is related to religion.

I called my grandfather Duck because that was what everyone else called him. I remember him as a hulk of a man who only wore bib overalls, under which was a shirt appropriate for the weather, and large, worn, dusty work boots. He didn't talk much, but when he did, you felt like you needed to listen to what he had to say.

This anecdote is not deep or intellectual; it is offered only to demonstrate that my life was one of discovery and continues to be that today.

Duck had a gold pocket watch, which he was pretty proud of, and must have shown it to me. Perhaps it was an award or simply a watch he inherited or purchased. He kept this prized possession in the top drawer of his dresser in his bedroom, a room carefully pointed out to me and my two brothers as off-limits to children.

While I have no recollection of a specific event, I assume Duck had shown me this watch and explained the inner workings of tiny and shiny gears, wheels, and springs, made up as watches were before the digital age. Perhaps he did this to educate me in mechanics, expecting me, like most males, to be fascinated by all things shiny and mechanical. It turns out he was more right than he imagined.

You probably have a good idea of where this story is going. Duck was off somewhere, perhaps fishing, one of his favorite pastimes. I mounted a chair and took the watch from his dresser. That violated rule number 1 — don't go in Duck's bedroom.

Far from improving anything, as I claim I like to do, I took the watch outside and placed it on one of the stepping stones leading to the outhouse, and using a hammer I had taken from the tool shed — broken rule number 2 — do not go into the tool shed without Duck, I hammered that watch until it revealed every one of its shiny gold secrets.

I sat there, fascinated by all those shimmering parts, which looked like tiny golden lace doilies scattered on the stone between my legs. At some point, it must have dawned on me what I had done, but at this point in life, my obfuscation skills were sorrowfully underdeveloped, so I just sat there admiring my discovery until my grandmother came along. I don't recall the specifics, but she must have hyperventilated when she saw the bling-littered stepping stone.

I also don't recall Duck's reaction to what I had done, but having seen his temper in the past, I can conclude he must have been furious. I have no memory of my punishment, although there must have been consequences. Duck, who made his living cutting granite blocks at a tombstone manufacturing company, was not a man to be trifled with.

Fortunately, I had the advantage of being the baby brother. My next older brother, Bob, was six years older, and my oldest brother, Bill, was ten years older than me, making them about ten and fourteen, respectively, at the time of my untimely (pun intended) misadventure. My grandmother had protected me from Duck's wrath on multiple occasions. My brothers probably suffered on my behalf and for their misdeeds at different times.

As you can tell by that last allegory, I was reverse engineering before age five. Most of the trouble I got into in my youth stemmed from my curiosity and questioning ways, not any desire to be destructive or break the rules just to break them.

This tendency to investigate the unknown extended to my religious training, which commenced when I moved to The Omaha Home for Boys, a home for displaced boys in Omaha, Nebraska.

I went to the Home a week or two shy of my fifth birthday. Set on top of what was referred to as "Inspiration Hill," it commanded an impressive view of the surrounding valleys and Fontenelle Park, which bordered the Home's property on the east.

The Home was larger than anything I had ever seen, larger than grandma's clapboard cottage and surrounding property. At the same time, being new construction with no grass yet growing and a series of boards laid down in the mud between buildings for walkways, it had a cold and derelict appearance.

I had no idea what was coming my way on that chilly September day when my grandmother summoned me to the living room. A stranger, a man, sat on our couch. He had thinning red hair and a ruddy complexion and seemed incredibly nervous, which transferred to me.

I recall a conversation but not the details. There may have been an effort to tell me what was happening, but in no way asking my consent. At some point, the man took me by one wrist, and my grandmother took hold of me by the other, and they dragged and carried me kicking and screaming to the old green woody station wagon the man had arrived in.

I would come to understand later that my grandmother was extremely ill with diabetes and could not take care of us three boys any longer. Thus, I joined my two older brothers, who had earlier disappeared from my life with no explanation that I remember, finding them at the Masonic Home for Boys, as it was called at that time.

The superintendent of the Home, the man who had come to take me from the warm embrace of my grandmother, was one John R. Glassy. Either an ordained, defrocked, or self-proclaimed minister, I was never sure which. I seem to recall he was Presbyterian and was often referred to by us boys as the Reverend or just the Rev, but never to his face.

Ours was a very Christian-Protestant upbringing in the best of the WASP traditions that dominated the Bible Belt then, as it does now. We said grace before each meal and prayed on our knees next to our beds at night, all the things you might expect growing up in the heart of Bible country.

The first building in which I lived was called the Buck Building. Four other buildings or dormitories for the boys were also named after benefactors who had donated a large sum of money to help build the Home in its new location.

Our housemother, Mrs. Stoft, a woman who could have been one of my boot camp Drill Instructors later in my life, required that we read and memorize Bible verses. Having something of a gift for memorization, a talent more than a bit timeworn by now, as my wife would attest, I could recite several Bible verses by the time I was eight.

I attended Sunday school each Sunday from age five to around age twelve or thirteen. At that time, I began to skip out of the indoctrination that was becoming more difficult for me to sit through without questioning both the logic and integrity of what was being taught to me and other children.

I confess to a degree of disappointment as my doubts about religion grew. The fantastic stories of voices emanating from a burning bush, or Shepherd's staff turning into a snake, the parting of waters with the wave of a hand, people returning from death, and Jesus feeding a host of people from a magic basket containing only a couple of fish and a few loaves of bread, were as exciting as any fairy tale I had ever read or heard.

As a child, you want to believe in miracles and magic. As I grew older and more skeptical, it was similar to discovering that there was no Santa Claus or Easter Bunny. Life was much more fun as long as you could cling to your fantasies. The letdown was palpable. We like to call that growing up unless it's about religion, then we become heretics.

At some point, around age ten, I read the Bible from cover to cover. That may have been prompted by an adult suggestion or my thirst for knowledge; I am no longer sure.

In the interest of honesty, I admit that I skimmed or jumped over the begat stuff both times that I read the so-called good book. After my first reading of the Bible, the questions piled up in my mind, and I began to voice those in earnest at every opportunity, primarily at church.

There seemed to be a good deal of violence in the Old Testament, along with dire threats of retribution for those who didn't follow the word of God as prescribed therein. Severe punishments for behaviors that today are quite common and accepted in most societies.

But in the New Testament, Jesus talks of turning the other cheek and presents a strikingly different vision of God. It seemed he should know since he purportedly was the son of God.

I began to ask questions in Sunday school, much to the dismay of the teachers, who I now believe were adults in the community volunteering their time to teach children what they had been taught to believe unquestionably about their particular religious affiliation.

In the conservative Midwest in the early 1950s, in the heart of the WASP world into which I had been born, a ten-year-old boy questioning his Sunday School teachers and the accuracy of the Bible was tantamount to heresy. It smacked of something right out of Rosemary's Baby, a movie that was still twenty years in the future.

I asked about the Bible stories that seemed highly improbable, if not impossible. I wondered why the stories depicted what appeared to be an angry and vindictive God calling for the death of various offenders in the Old Testament. At the same time, Jesus preached that his Father would forgive all who believed in Him in the New Testament.

Even the least religious among us surely has heard the story of Cain killing his brother Abel in a fit of religious jealousy. God sends a plague on the Pharaoh and his family. God kills every man, woman, and child in Sodom and Gomorrah. God decides to kill Moses because his son has not been circumcised, although the details behind this particular anecdote seem a bit fuzzy. And, of course, there is the great flood He called down upon the world to destroy all He had made, save one older man who purportedly built an ark big enough to weather the storm and hold two of every animal that made our planet their Home.

I am sorry, but if God were a world leader behaving today as he did in the Old Testament, the United Nations would have him up on charges of crimes against humanity. The list of horrors He rained down on his subjects is long and would make the Brothers Grimm grimace, and probably, it did; it may have inspired some of their gruesome fairytales.

My questions about these, and many other stories, along with my questions about why these events had only happened during one short period over 2,000 years ago, not before or since, and not in the modern world, not in any world, were problematic. These questions went unanswered and were not welcome in classrooms meant to shape the unquestioned thinking of young minds. Had I chosen to check out a Catholic Church, an exorcism would likely have been in order.

As I grew older and pondered the mysteries of religion, I would understand the oxymorons between the Old and New Testaments. It was the evolution of religion at work. The Old Testament, at least the first five books, was written some 1,200 to 1,600 years before the birth of Jesus. Attributed in large part to Moses, who is supposed to have personally heard from God, they espoused a belief (a) by one man and (b) for a time much different than the world Jesus would be born to, let alone that of our modern world.

As I became more aware of fundamentalism and terrorism, terms that became a part of everyday life for most of us in the late 20th and early 21st century, I could see parallels in the thinking of fundamentalists subscribing to orthodoxies, whether Christian, Jew, Islam or any other religion.

Adherents are taught to close their minds to anything but a narrow interpretation of the written word. This type of groupthink or brainwashing often produces horrible consequences, encouraging adherents to despise or at least dislike those who do not share their zealotry. A harshness and rigidity of thought hardens the mind to anything but dogma.

My Christian Sunday school experience, I now see, bore a striking resemblance to some but not all the Islamic Madrasas where unfortunate young Muslims are taught one version of Islam and the Qur'an, and one quite different from what other Muslims believe. They learn of a worldview often twisted by the adults grooming a generation of fundamentalists, continually telling them not to question or look beyond their teachings for answers. They are to follow the word mindlessly.

I mentioned having read the Bible twice as a young boy. The second time was at the behest of a local minister who had come to the Boys Home one Sunday afternoon to express his concerns about me, my questions, and I suspect my endangered soul, to our minister and superintendent, the Reverend John R. Glassy.

By this time, I might point out that I had changed churches several times. Each Sunday morning, we were loaded on the Home's bus (originally a Diamond-T truck) and taken to the downtown area of the Benson district of Omaha.

There was a clutch of churches within several blocks of each other: Presbyterian, Lutheran, Episcopalian, Methodist, and Catholic. I don't recall whether there were any Jewish Synagogues, but I'm confident there were no Mosques. I would not have known what they were back then if they did exist. The religious educators were careful to stick to their scripts.

I started in the Presbyterian Sunday school at age five and was stuck there for a time because I was still relatively small, and there was always someone responsible for looking after me and making decisions for me. I was deposited there and told to stay put until someone gathered me for the return trip to the Home. I wasn't free at that young and tender age to choose where to spend Sunday mornings. I wouldn't have known what to do except chase butterflies.

At some point, around the time I completed my first reading of the Bible, around age twelve, the disillusionment began to set up like curing plaster. After a couple of birthdays had passed, I switched to being either a Lutheran or Methodist; I no longer recall which. After a time, I changed to another church to continue searching for greater meaning in what was being taught. I never tried the Episcopalian or Catholic religions because their conservatism and the Catholic costumes scared the hell out of me — most likely their intent.

It didn't matter which temple I attended. Despite the variety of colorful vestments, the consuming of or abstention from wine at communion, and all the trappings inside and out that defined one church or another, I kept finding much the same dogma, words designed to bind your mind, accompanied by the same dire threats of condemnation and an eternity in hell for not adhering to one ideology or another. While preaching the love of Jesus, they held the threat of the Old Testament burning hell over your head.

The Inquisition

I was around thirteen when I was summoned to the Administration Building at the Home on that Sunday afternoon in the fall. Two men, Glassy and the minister from whichever hallowed institution I was attending at the time, sat somberly on the green leather sofa in the living room. Nothing burned in the darkened fireplace—they were only for decoration in most of the buildings, a practice I still don't understand.

They motioned me to a matching green leather chair across from them. Glassy cleared his throat, his steely eyes peering into my very soul. Then, they voiced their concerns about my obvious rejection of the general teachings of Christianity, suggesting that I read the Bible. I explained that I had read the Bible, which had given rise to many of my questions to begin with.

I am sure that answer did not please Glassy or the Reverend. With a perceptible flushing of facial color to an even deeper red than usual, Glassy recommended that I reread the Bible. Though his guidance was in the form of a suggestion, his tone was more like an order.

So, I read the Bible a second time. I must admit I may have read it this second time more to confirm my considerable doubts than to expect to find some revelation or enlightenment. In any case, it did nothing to alter my growing conviction that the stories in the Bible were mostly myths made up by some very pious, ignorant, and frightened people, and mostly men—check that, exclusively men.

Many myths and legends are probably based in some small part on reality, or what the weavers of these tales believed to be reality at the time. A legend is a story that's purported to be historical in nature, but that is without substantiation. Legend also refers to anything that inspires a body of stories or anything of lasting importance or fame. The story is handed down orally but continues to evolve with time.

King Arthur, Blackbeard, and Robin Hood are quite possibly based on real people who, while not as flamboyant and chivalrous as the legends, were nevertheless admirable people. Over the years of telling and retelling the stories of real people, these legends grew.

In the case of the Bible, the authors were likely convinced that all the stories passed down to them over the years were fact. Stories of mythical figures and miraculous occurrences, many of which we know today to be natural phenomena. Things like the parting of the sea. We know today that receding oceans can be the result of an inverted storm surge, a "negative surge." Severe storms can cause dramatic pressure changes. Reduced pressure pushing down on the ocean causes the ocean to expand upwards, resulting in rising water. Sea surface levels can drop when pressure increases, resulting in a negative surge.

"With the water dispersed, the Israelites were able to walk on dry ground and cross the sea, followed by the Egyptian army. Once the Israelites have safely crossed, Moses drops his staff, closing the sea and drowning the pursuing Egyptians."

Could it have happened as it was written, or did people see this natural phenomenon? As they wove their tales of the Jews escaping the Egyptians over the centuries, might the parting of the seas have become an imagined part of their harrowing tale? Though they probably lived too far south to see an aurora borealis, what might they have thought of that? They wanted to believe in the mystical or divine more than anything, even more than life itself.

Nothing more was ever said to me about my faith, or lack thereof, at the boys' Home. Still, I detected an increased coldness, even anger, toward me by the Reverend Glassy right up to the time he was finally dismissed for reasons never made public. An exhaustive search of the history of the boys' Home produced no mention of Glassy, a man you must have spent nearly ten years there as the superintendent.

It was rumored, however, and suspected that it was due to his cruel treatment of the older boys and the staff. Like the stories in the Bible, there was likely at least a germ of truth to the rumor. Glassy was never thought of as a Steiff Teddy Bear by anyone I knew, including a significant number of the staff.

By around age fifteen, I was more or less convinced that the Bible was a work of fiction, or perhaps wishful thinking by the various authors and revisionists over the almost two millennia it has existed, as opposed to a historical account of anything. I should mention that when I refer to the Bible, I'm talking about the Christian Bible, with the understanding that the Old Testament comes from the Torah, also known as the Five Books of Moses and the Chumash.

I had learned to keep my questions to myself, given their shock value in Nebraska, where protestant beliefs were deeply embedded in society. I witnessed how often questions of Christian beliefs became the fodder for angry responses from a sometimes emotional religious adult community. Any suggestion from me that the word of God may have sprung from the imaginings of confused and uneducated older men proved to be terrifying, and I suppose threatening, to people of faith. The critical thinking proffered by the Ancient Greeks, like Socrates, was not taught where these people were schooled in religion.

A brief comment or two about critical thinking: it is one of the most important and underused capabilities of the evolved human mind, and is responsible in large part for our evolution beyond being instinctual herd animals.

Socrates is credited with at least codifying critical thinking. Long before Socrates, as we evolved into a higher form of thinking beings, our brains began to examine, question, and attempt to understand the world in which we lived. But Socrates, perhaps more than anyone else in history, put it in terms that made sense to the rest of us.

Socrates, generally considered one of the founders of Western philosophy, set the agenda for the tradition of critical thinking. He defined the process of reflectively questioning common beliefs and explanations. He advocated for distinguishing between those beliefs that are reasonable and logical from those which, however appealing they may be to our sense of understanding and well-being or however much they might serve our ideology and our personal interests, if they lack adequate evidence or rational foundation to warrant belief they must be at least suspect if not rejected. Put more simply, if something sounds too good to be true, chances are it is not.

This hard-core examination of what sounds or feels good is not always a convenient way to deal with the world around us. Life is so much easier when you can blindly accept the explanations of others, those you consider your superiors, spiritual, or political leaders. It allows us to return to whatever mundane pursuits that give us pleasure rather than go to the trouble of understanding life's mysteries. Deferring understanding and decision-making to others allows us to avoid making what are often difficult choices and mistakes. Let the leaders make mistakes; we can criticize them for the results.

Back to the story of my journey away from religion. After my run-in with the minister and the Reverend John R., it would be another eight years or so before I had another meaningful discussion on theology. That opportunity would come when my first wife, Mary, who was an Irish Catholic, wanted us to marry in the Catholic Church. She and her family encouraged me to become a Catholic so that could happen.

Doing so frankly meant little more than joining a Moose or Elk lodge. That is not meant to demean the Catholic Church or fraternities in any way. It reflects my state of mind, then and now. Nevertheless, my curiosity about Catholicism made attending adult Catechism an enjoyable, if not an altogether transforming experience. This was one of the churches I avoided as a child based on what appeared to me to be a conservative and, at times, severe view of the world due to the Catholic dogma and some scary-ass black outfits sported by the clergy. I would now have the opportunity to explore the unknown, something I have always enjoyed and continue to do to this day.

I will repeat the following refrain more than a few times: I am not bashing religion despite my critical reviews of its practices. At least, that is not my intent. I question some of the stories and the history often professed to be fact, yes, but I am not bashing anyone's beliefs. Religion, in general, became a philosophy I found seriously flawed and lacking in meaning in my life.

The one-night-a-week adult catechism class at Saint Mary's went on for several weeks, six as I recall, and the experience was heightened for me by the young priest who taught the class. The young priest had radically modern ideas in the early 1960s that may have been his undoing a few years later.

Father Schwab was well over six feet tall, skinny as a beanpole. He loved fast cars and had a marvelous sense of humor, not the sort of thing I expected from a Priest based on my experiences with the dour deacons in the Protestant churches I had visited.

Among the things he enjoyed doing was donning his cape and hiding in the halls of St. Mary's school to step out from a corner in a hallway filled with elementary students hurrying to class to scare the crap out of them with his Dracula impression. I assume they all came through those experiences with a minimum of trauma or any discernible psychological scars.

Father Schwab won me over on the first night of class as a friend and a straight shooter. He struck me as a man of uncommon common sense when, in the course of discussing some of the common misconceptions about Catholicism, he said that many people's perceptions of Catholicism were all a load of bullshit or some other comparable noun. There was an audible and collective chorus of gasps from the class of twenty adults, who were a tad more pious than myself. I know I smiled if I didn't outright laugh at his comment.

Schwab went on to explain that profanity, in all its many colorful and sometimes uncomfortable forms, was the construct of humans and that nowhere in the Bible will you find references to profanity or a list of forbidden words in any category. Take that, FCC – not even God made a list of forbidden words.

That is just one example of why I came to like the man. Father Schwab and I became casual friends who discussed theology over a glass of Guinness and across the pool table in the rectory a time or two. He seemed as anxious to examine my resistance to religion as I was to understand how people could accept what I believed then and still believe to be some pretty outrageous tales.

As I raised the same questions I had raised as a child, Schwab acknowledged the legitimacy of my questions and could only state that no one could prove or disprove much of the Bible. Or, for that matter, the existence of God. He said that it came down to a deep well of faith. Either you had it, or you didn't.

The good Father Schwab will always hold a special place in my memory for his sense of humor, imagination, and honesty; in some ways, he smoothed my path to Atheism. He was a better pool player than I was, but most people are.

That sense of humor, or more accurately his willingness to speak his mind, may have derailed or at least delayed his career in the Catholic Church, and certainly at St. Mary's in Omaha.

I was not privy to all the details, but the diocese of St. Mary's was one of the larger parishes in Omaha and an apparent coup for any priest. When the reigning diocese Monsignor died, I think Schwab thought the post was or should have been his based on his tenure there, but someone in the Church hierarchy brought in a priest from another parish to fill the post; politics seems to exist everywhere. I know Schwab was not happy, and I have to believe he expressed that displeasure up and down the halls of the Catholic congress in Omaha.

The last I heard or saw of Father Schwab, he was being transferred to a small parish somewhere in North Dakota, which, I believe, was the equivalent of exile for challenging the hierarchy's authority and decision-making. I truly hope he landed on his feet and achieved, at least, most of what he sought in the priesthood; he was one of the good guys.

Speaking his mind and challenging the reigning authorities of the time was also Jesus' undoing, so my friend who enjoyed that deep well of faith must have felt he was in good company.

At this point in my story, I am in my early twenties, and my basic philosophies and beliefs are in full bloom, as I believe happens to most people by that age. We tend to firm our positions on most matters by about twenty or so.

It is my opinion, and it is one that garnered me an A in psychology, that by about age twenty—the exact age varies with each individual—our basic philosophies and beliefs about life are well-centered and established. Barring some overwhelming evidence to the contrary or a significant emotional event such as a near-death experience that rocks our world and brings on a full-blown reassessment of what we believe, we will remain mostly who we are for the rest of our lives.

That doesn't mean you or I can't be influenced by a strong argument, or more so by evidence. I learn something new every day and often tweak my philosophy based on new information. But opinions, conjecture, and fairy tales won't make that happen, and nothing I have heard from those who advocate for religion has offered anything more than one of the nouns mentioned above.

Who, what, when, where, and why? The five Ws. Those are the touchstones of good journalism. However, it appears less and less critical to our modern media, where ratings and advertising dollars drive survival, and the talking heads are not reluctant to take sides on issues. The days of wizened little old men printing a newspaper in their basement to put out what they see as the truth, men who would then stand on the street corner in sweltering heat or freezing snow to hand out their papers, appear long gone. The likes of Edward R. Morrow and Sam Donaldson are now found only in history books. The modern journalist is closer to an entertainer than a journalist or newscaster.

We do have social media, podcasts, and blogs out the wazoo, but few of those salute any form of journalistic standards. It's all about garnering followers, ratings, and advertising dollars. Still, when you answer these five 'W' questions, you get closer to the truth than you can by relying on rumor, innuendo, or mythology.

Those Ws are also at the heart of criminal investigations. Investigators are invariably eager to discover how, where, when, and why a crime occurred. That knowledge will almost always lead them to the one they are seeking.

For my purposes here, in understanding the evolution of religion, I have decided to begin with the why of it all. Most of us don't choose to do anything unless we answer the question: why should I do that? Or why should I accept that? It is common when someone asks you to join them in some adventure to say, "Why not?" Inviting someone to give a good reason for not taking up the challenge helps us decide. Asking the why question is a primary human filter for making decisions in life and, I believe, perhaps the most important word in human language that has motivated us in discovery and propelled us forward as a species.

When we see the all-too-often real-life horrific crimes in the news or on the Internet, we will typically ask, "Why would anyone do that?" When investigating a crime, the police often seek a motive. Why would anyone commit such and such a crime? Knowing why someone does something frequently leads to unraveling any mystery and, in the case of a crime, contributes to the profile of a possible suspect. Examining why we needed or felt we needed religion seems an appropriate starting point for this exploration.

I plan to insert a fictional account or story here and there to suggest how events might have played out as we journeyed from the Stone Age to the present. I hope they help visualize our possible path to religion.

In closing this section, I feel obligated to say once again that I am not against religion, nor do I hold any hatred toward those who practice one religion or another. Do I have a problem with some of the pain inflicted on innocent people down through the centuries by religious zealots, excesses that continue today? Of course, I do. But I understand that extremists exist in all facets of humanity and have done so from the beginning of time. These fringe lunatics - I have no kinder or definitive adjective to describe them - these people who live at the extremes of any issue no more represent all of humanity or a given religion than a rabid dog defines all canines on the planet.

Why Religion?

The time to examine the why of our search has arrived. There are as many answers to that question as there have been people throughout history, but it still demands reflection and examination.

To understand the why of religion, we need to travel back in time, way back, down through history, well before recorded history, at least in so far as our imagination permits us to do so. So, join me in our time machine as we travel back to a time before the ancient civilizations of Greece, Babylon, Egypt, and the Roman Empire. We're going back to before the advent of writing and recording the human experience on this planet.

Let's set the date of our time machine for 50,000 years before Jesus was born, the era the Christians have dubbed as BCE (Before the Common Era). Interestingly, this term used to be just BC - Before Christ. Christians had concluded that the only thing that mattered was life after Jesus had spoken. By the 17th century, BCE was in use. Christians claimed the change was an attack on Christianity. The reality is just the opposite. BC was Christians imposing their beliefs on the rest of the planet when, in fact, Christians make up less than one-third of the people on our marvelous Earth.

Our time machine has landed in 50,000 BCE. Language and writing appear to have developed between 35,000 and 50,000 years ago, as evidenced by cave paintings from the period of the Crow-Magnon Man (c. 50,000-30,000 BCE), which appear to express concepts concerning daily life. These images suggest a language because, in some instances, they seem to tell a story (say, of a hunting expedition in which specific events occurred) rather than simply pictures of animals and people. Before that, we painted static images on cave walls and spit paint to outline our hands on rocks. The written word appeared around 3500

BCE. This early writing was called cuneiform and consisted of making specific marks in wet clay with a reed implement. That's enough history for now.

We have landed somewhere in Africa or maybe Eurasia. The era referred to as the Middle Paleolithic Age, more commonly referred to as the Stone Age, as opposed to the entire Paleolithic era, covering a million years of our history. For our exploration, we have chosen to drop closer to the end of that period. Rest assured, this is not an advertisement for the Paleo diet. I'm almost as cynical of that diet as I am of theology.

The period we're in is called the Third Interglacial period. Great ice caps spread south from the polar region and then receded over vast parts of Europe and Western Asia. The saber-toothed tiger is destined for extinction. Hippopotamus, Rhinos, mammoths, and elephants graze across the Great Plains of Europe.

Many animals retreated southward as the air over the land mass cooled with the advancing ice caps. Small bands of men, along with women and children, those we call Homo neanderthalensis, and maybe other forms of sub-humans, the ancestors of Homo neanderthalensis, still wander the land, leaving scarce examples of their existence save a few flint instruments turned up by farmers tilling that same land over the ensuing centuries. Eventually, archaeologists searching for the story of human history will begin to assemble the puzzle of our beginnings, a job that continues today.

It's time for a fictional story.

Great mounds of dark gray clouds move across the skies as our tribe moves down the trail, following the path the Chief and his advisors have decided to take. As the light of day leaves, it is time to find a location for food and shelter. The warriors, one in the lead, two on both flanks of the group, and the two bringing up the rear, watch for predators searching for an easy meal; we are all on full alert.

The wind blows gently from the north, and the protectors of our tribe stop briefly, turning their heads to sample the air for the scent of the big cats or any other animals that they know are watching us from the cover of the forests.

The Chief walks ahead of the women, children, and older men but well behind the lead warrior. He is safe there from all but the fiercest attacks. The tribe knows they have to protect the wisest of our clan.

The children are bundled in fur, but still feel the bitter cold. Everyone except the warriors, who must stay vigilant, walks with their heads down as they knife through the wind with their bodies, blindly following the leaders to our next encampment.

The women scour the ground as they walk, looking for any edible scrap they can scoop up and put into the bag hanging from their waists. They look for the perfect rock or piece of slate that can be later fashioned into a tool for scraping fur, making fire, or any of the many jobs that will fall to them once we have stopped for the night.

End of story

Archeological evidence shows that these ancient people mastered fire to survive the cold temperatures, including the knowledge that cave shelters were preferable to huddling around a fire on the open plain. From all the evidence found to date, they were capable hunters, made their clothing, and were generally on the evolutionary path to modern humans.

While we can confidently say that our ancient relatives were unsophisticated by today's standards, they weren't stupid or wouldn't have survived a challenging and dangerous world.

I wouldn't be here reading this, nor could you listen to me without their struggles and subsequent evolution. None of us would be here. We would all be in pools of tar and oil along with the dinosaurs.

Recent research suggests these roving bands had an impressive array of tools and were knowledgeable enough about their territory to select strategic areas to live and hunt. At the same time, it is safe to say that while they may have had the sense to come in from the rain, they had no concept of how the rain occurred or anything about the phenomena of weather such as thunder, lightning, tornadoes, or blizzards, all manner of things that we understand today. Likely, they cowered in their caves during such violent events.

Story-time - an anecdote

The fall air was crisp, and winter was approaching. The trees, ablaze with gold, orange, and red leaves, were preparing to enter their winter sleep. While our people recognized the physical changes of the seasons around them and made the necessary preparations for the harsh winter, they did not understand why the leaves changed, or why it snowed and rained.

In our clan, Hamel and Mambe, ten- and eight-year-old brothers, ran and played just outside the mouth of the cave, jousting with sticks and racing to see who could climb a tree the fastest, as did all the boys in our tribe. While the boys played at these activities, acquiring the skills they would need to survive in a threatening world, their mothers kept a cautious vigil.

A large cougar on a nearby boulder, with golden eyes that never blinked or wavered, watched our boys play. The muscles in the giant cat's haunches throbbed with the prospect of a hunt as it crouched low on the big rock to instinctively minimize its profile, its coat blending with the gray-brown of the monolithic stone.

The boy's mothers, grasping large clubs with callus-covered hands made strong from years of hard labor, placed themselves between the cougar's line of sight and our boys at play. The mothers met the gaze of the big cat with the same intensity as that of the big cat.

If the cougar moved to get a clear line of sight of the boys and perhaps an angle of attack, the women shifted with the cougar's piercing stare, letting the big cat know that it was being watched and that there would be a fierce battle and a painful price to pay for it trying to take one of our babies.

The wind blew a dried tumbleweed across the ground. The mothers saw it in their peripheral vision, glancing only long enough to verify it was no threat, then immediately making eye contact with the big cat again.

The younger men of the tribe were away hunting for food, leaving the women, children, older people, and a couple of young men behind for security. The local predators, having observed our tribe's behavior and our comings and goings for a long time, knew their best chance to make a meal of one of us was when the warriors were away.

Hamel, a bit smaller and faster than his brother, Mambe, smacked Mambe a little too hard with a stick. Mambe glared at Hamel.

"Do that again, and I'll beat you till you can't walk!"

Mambe did his best to imitate the men in our clan who talked to each other like this as they established the clan hierarchy. Neither boy paid any attention to the cougar, secure in the knowledge that their mothers were standing guard.

"Sorry,"

Hamel feigned submission, but with a perceptible lack of sincerity. He wasn't all that sorry because Mambe always used his physical advantage to bully Hamel. Conversely, Hamel almost always won out in a battle of wits. He was a better politician and negotiator than Mambe and knew when to back down and when to stand and fight. Both boys were developing traits that would serve them well one day as adults in our clan.

As darkness enveloped their world, denying them the crucial definitions of the world around them that allowed them to avoid danger, the mothers called to the children to get inside the cave and around the fire for the night.

End of story

Fast-forward about 45,000 years. My, how time flies. Mambe and Hamel have long since turned to dust. Perhaps modern archeologists will one day discover their bones. The "cave people" have faded far into the past, virtually unknown to the modern human species of 5,000 years ago.

Ancient Greece is approaching the Bronze Age. The Chinese are farming the Yellow River Valley using stone tools and weapons. The Roman Empire is still some 4,500 years into the future. Even the Egyptian Empire is 2,000 years away from its impressive existence. We humans have made progress, but we are still a very primitive species by today's standards.

There is some evidence that early humans observed rituals attending death, possibly as far back as 50,000 years ago. Archeologists have found graves in more recent times that indicate some effort by the people 19,000 years ago to honor those who had died. The Red Lady, a famous cave in Spain, shows evidence of being a burial chamber.

Sometimes, people were buried with belongings or food, suggesting that people must have imagined, or perhaps hoped, that something happened to you after death, that death was not the end, but rather a transition or journey to another place. Whether 20,000 years ago, they had anything approaching religion as we know it today is unknowable since they could not write anything down. Writing in the form of pictographs was still many years into the future.

The people of that time hadn't been exposed to the teachings of modern religion, so what was in their minds? We can't know, but what must be drawn from these ritualistic burials is that these societies wanted to believe there was something after death, an idea that likely persisted for many thousands of years before these people dug the graves for their loved ones who had died, or tucked them away in the back of a cave.

We do know that animals fear death in general. That is why they run away from death when pursued by a predator. But do they have any concept of life after death? If not, then what spawns the fear of death in animals and humans? For humans, was it losing what these ancients had presently that drove them to distraction when thinking of their deaths? What did life mean to these early humans? What does life mean to an animal?

Since we evolved from animals, perhaps we carry this fear from a million years ago somewhere deep in what some scientists call our reptilian brains.

Like modern man, these ancients wanted to live on, even with life as hard and treacherous as it must have been back then. Life was still seen as precious, and few welcomed death, either their own or that of a loved one.

It would be simple to say these Stone Age beings practiced religion, but that would be tantamount to insisting that elephants mourning their dead have a sense of a higher power. There are persistent stories of penguins in Antarctica burying their dead. Are they practicing religion? There is no question that both of these species have been observed engaging in rituals surrounding death, a type of mourning of lost members of their tribe, but do they have or practice a religion of any kind? Are we, as humans, and the only ones created in the image of God according to our mythology, prepared to make an argument that perhaps animals do believe in an afterlife? I would guess not.

Our human pursuit of superiority and dominance of all that is non-human, due in part to the teachings by many religions that we are made in God's image like no other creation of God, would not allow our minds to go to such lengths; what could we possibly eat if we believed that? That would strip us of our unique and dominant god-like status in the animal kingdom. Who exactly was created in God's image if animals other than humans engage in religious thought and ritual?

These Stone Agers of long ago were more closely related to their animal cousins in understanding the world around them than they are to modern humans. Modern man is far removed from that era as we struggle to unravel and understand our ancient ancestors. The fact is, something was going on back then, but we can never know with any certainty precisely what that might have been.

As hunter-gatherers, we had witnessed death. We had killed other animals for food. We had seen the light go out in their eyes as they slipped into the darkness of death. While we may not have understood death, we understood extinguishing life in a living species. How did those experiences influence our thoughts and fears about our death and the deaths of those around us?

We can't know what was going on in the minds of ancient humans any more than we can understand the workings of the minds of animals in today's modern world. We can only speculate based on finding the bones and remnants of their civilization and putting our modern thought process and spin on those findings.

Any theories we might entertain are inevitably distorted through the filters of our modern minds, warped to a degree by the very evolution that has brought us to this point in our existence, both our social and religious evolution. Those filters will give each of us a different interpretation of that history, another phenomenon that can be explained.

I listened to a psychologist long ago explain how two individuals could see and hear the same thing but tell two different versions of events. The police deal with this all the time when interviewing witnesses. Ten people can witness the same crime and give ten different descriptions of the perpetrator.

The speaker characterized each of us as traveling through life with this large, curved lens we hold up between us and the rest of the world. Everything we see and experience must pass through this lens to reach our senses, telling us what we see, hear, feel, or fear.

As each of us experiences life in our unique way, those experiences reshape our personal lenses, like an optician grinding lenses for your glasses or contacts. Since no two of us have precisely the same experiences, our lenses are shaped quite differently from those around us. This distorts or shapes our interpretation of life, events, and the emotions we experience. We put our unique spin on what we see and hear.

That is why I said that our assumptions about the ancients are based on our experiences to date and thousands of years and billions of human experiences over our time on this planet. All of this has shaped the lens so that our view is distorted. The best we can do is speculate on what might have been happening without written historical records to guide us.

This same analogy could explain some of the Bible's apparent contradictions and the interpretations of some of its alleged events. Each person who contributed to the writings of religion saw, heard, and felt the stories told through their unique lens. Just a note—virtually everything written in religious texts was written long after the events supposedly happened. The authors were not eyewitnesses.

Yes, religion has been evolving and continues to do so based on advances in human knowledge and experiences. There was no clap of thunder or a flash of lightning, and suddenly, we had what we today call religion.

Contrary to the theory—and it is a theory if not a myth—that God created the universe in a week's time, scientific evidence points to a very different process that has gone on for billions of years.

What we believe today in terms of slavery, women, witches, animal sacrifices, and a litany of often confounding issues that were accepted in biblical times is very different from what people believed 500 years ago, which was very different from what humans knew and believed 2,000 years ago. And human beliefs will be dramatically different 500 years from now. Our descendants will look back at us in bewilderment and, most likely, a degree of humor at what we declared to be the facts about life and the universe in which we live.

Why did religion rise and evolve to be the force it is today? In a word, fear. Think about those ancient humans huddling in their caves, fearing everything in their world that they didn't understand. Since they understood practically nothing about the world they inhabited, save the need for food and shelter, and even some of that was potentially dangerous, they had to be the poster children for post-traumatic stress disorder.

From what we know, they could not have imagined our solar system, let alone the entire universe. Their whole world consisted of the distances they could move on foot. Minor changes in the weather drove them to cover, and the origins of the weather must have been a complete mystery to them.

Of course, they learned to adapt to climate, just as all animals do, wearing furs and seeking shelter from the cold and storms, but truly understanding their world was still millennia away.

They learned where to find game to eat and perhaps to follow migrating game. They learned where to forage for fruits and roots, foods they instinctively craved for their diet. Most animals in the wild do the same thing, much the way a bear moves up and down a mountainside, as the seasons dictate where food will be the most plentiful.

While they did learn to create fire and knew how to use that, as well as some rudimentary stone tools, these ancients had yet to progress all that far beyond their animal cousins.

Imagine the fear in the minds of ancient people when blizzards, earthquakes, eclipses, and meteor showers visited their small world. It is not difficult to visualize them cowering in their caves during a massive windstorm, with great trees falling all around or tornadoes ripping up giant trees and tossing them around like the twigs these people threw into a fire.

Add to this world of flying and falling objects that could kill them. The ravages of disease and other illnesses blew out the candle of life in a loved one or a member of the tribe. How could this happen? How could someone seem to be vibrant and healthy one day and on their deathbed the next? These were the unfathomable mysteries of the ancient ones.

One thing that is obvious to even the casual observer is that fear, especially traumatic fear, can drive people to some pretty extreme behaviors to avoid whatever it is they fear. Even with our advanced knowledge of the universe we live in, we can still be driven to distraction by fears, real or imagined.

For example, look at the United States in the 1950s during the height of the Cold War when we were engaged in a full-tilt nuclear arms race with the Soviet Union. People were driven to distraction, building bomb shelters and stocking food and guns in the belief that if Armageddon did come in the form of a nuclear holocaust (a belief based on the religions of many), they might survive to repopulate the Earth like a bunch of Adams and Eves.

Many people believed then, and some still do, that the Bible predicted just such an ending with the world being consumed by fire. The generation living during the nuclear arms race was convinced in their minds that an all-out nuclear war with the Soviet Union was inevitable and would, in fact, result in the final judgment. Almost seventy years later, the good news is that they were misguided, and we are still here, and the Soviet Union is not.

Today, we have other survivalists who are convinced that our government, defined as the progressives or liberals by the conservative right-wing, will go rogue on us, turning our country into a police state. These conspiracy-manic people are engaged in a media strategy of incendiary propaganda against our government. All the while, they are stockpiling arms so they can take over and create their version of a police state.

They equate everything but guns and living off the land with some communist conspiracy. What is most interesting is that their general political and social philosophy, often described as libertarian, were they to be in control, would likely see them using autocratic methods.

Libertarian is typically defined as no government interference, and everyone is free to do as they please. A most recent example of this libertarian approach to life is the refusal of many people to be vaccinated against COVID-19. In the face of a pandemic, and with the miracles of modern medicine, these people still refused to believe the government was trying to help them, and many, perhaps tens of thousands, died for their misguided beliefs. Their myopic approach to society endangered tens of thousands more around them.

You will find that many, if not most, of these people are devout Christians and sometimes fanatical Christians, which most often means they are opposed to gays and gay marriage and abortion, and they dislike people of color. They seem intent on vilifying non-Christians. And they are typically strong nationalist who are opposed to immigration, especially by people of color.

Given the power to rule the country, it seems likely these conservatives would use that power to oppress masses of people they either disagreed with or disliked, so much for being a libertarian. It sounds more like an authoritarian and theocratic approach to me.

Like our nuclear Chicken Littles of the 1950s, some of these people have bunkers in the woods, also stockpiled with food and weapons—weapons are big with this group—that they believe will protect them against a military of several million government warriors with state-of-the-art weapons, tanks, fighter jets, and whatever else this fantasy boogeyman of a government might throw at them. I think they have watched too many Bruce Willis films.

The truth is, if this ever did happen, the odds are probably about seven to one against it happening - assuming 50 million nutcases out of 330 million people. We all have a better chance of winning the lottery three times in a row than defeating the military might of the United States. Add to that millions of armed, hungry citizens roaming the planet looking for food who don't embrace the libertarian philosophy, and these folks are screwed.

The other thing on our side that is hopeful is nearly 300 years of democracy and the knowledge by our leaders that we, the people, would never tolerate such an act of insurgency. Add a commitment by many in government to protect the freedoms established and guaranteed by our Constitution, including the First Amendment to the Constitution that states, "Congress shall make no law respecting an establishment of religion, or prohibiting the free exercise thereof;..." and the odds are in our favor that we keep our democracy.

If the survivalist's worst dreams were to come true, there would be roaming bands of homeless, hungry, and desperate people. You and I, who don't side with the far right and millions of others in both political parties, many with guns, would far outnumber what the survivalists have.

This political rant is meant to point out the extremes to which we can be prodded by fear of the unknown or the imagined, even with all our advancements in science and technology. Our ancient ancestors were no different. Faced with overwhelming fears, they sought protection from those fears and likely got that from believing in higher powers.

What happens in the human mind that takes us to such extreme beliefs and behavior? As I write this, I have read of studies of the human brain as scientists and psychologists attempt to understand how religion stimulates certain parts of the brain and turns one person into a fundamentalist. At the same time, another, like me, becomes an atheist. All the while, the majority of us keep our heads screwed on right and reject the extreme ideas of the religious zealots.

No, I do not consider atheism to be extreme, although that realm of thought is still in the minority, but a growing minority. One significant difference between us free thinkers and the indoctrinated religious fundamentalists is that we are not trying to force others to think the way we do under the threat of violence. We will argue the merits or demerits of religion until we're blue in the face over a glass of beer, after which we will hug you and wish you well. I'm afraid I can't say the same for most religious zealots.

I am trying to point out that fear, real, imagined, or taught, can drive us to distraction. Is it any wonder that the ancients began to believe that some superhuman entity was behind every violent act of nature? Look at modern man when tornadoes, cyclones, hurricanes, and tsunamis devastate our world. With all our knowledge and technology, we are still helpless against a 9.0 earthquake, a Category 5 hurricane, or a Category 5 tornado.

After such a disaster, many of us turn to our religions and our God, seeking an explanation for these events, for answers to why people, perhaps our relatives or friends, were killed and their homes destroyed. We take solace in believing that every event is part of God's mysterious plan, that He (or She) has some grand plan for human life on Earth. In that regard, it would seem we have not traveled all that far from our ancient ancestor's state of paranoia.

If we can divorce ourselves from the emotional aspects of religion, the why of an evolving belief in some higher or mystical being is obvious.

The Gods

The Neanderthals, hanging out about 40,000 years ago, and maybe even humans before that, having none of the scientific understanding of events we possess today and trying to comprehend a major disaster along with the loss of loved ones, give us the recipe for the belief that a God or gods were behind the horrible events that befell them.

Back then, multiple gods were thought to rule the world and be responsible for good and bad life events. But why gods? Where should this idea of a supreme, omnipotent being come from in the minds of these simplistic and backward people? Let us look at some possibilities.

Logic would suggest that within a tribe of humans back then, as with any animals that run in packs, a pride, conspiracy, dazzles, or the troops we see today, some members were stronger, braver, and wiser than all the others. There must have been fierce hunters and warriors who faced up to the largest beast, seemingly unafraid, even if they were pooping their bear skins. There were wise men and women whose comprehension of some of the challenges and complexities of a Stone Age world far surpassed that of the ordinary tribal members. These individuals became the leaders, enforcers, pharmacists, and the revered ones.

This recognition, by the tribe at large, of superior physical attributes and intellects within their clan must have led to elevating those people to a position of influence and authority, just as happens today. They became the leaders among their kind, almost god-like, one would suspect, with all the trappings and privileges that might have attended ancient royalty. The people recognized that some in their tribe excelled in different pursuits.

We see this elevation of the strongest and brightest to the highest levels play out in any species and any society throughout the animal kingdom today and within our political and economic structure. Sometimes, these individuals are elevated by the members of society, and sometimes, they get there either by force of will or some skulduggery. Either way, they ascend to positions of power.

Observations and history suggest the survival of any group of individuals depends on developing this hierarchy. The opposite would be anarchy with no one in charge, an experiment that has failed time and time again throughout history. While some anarchical states existed, they have yet to be sustainable over the long term. As you listen to this reading, anarchy is playing out in countries like Haiti and Jamaica, with roaming gangs of wannabe warlords fighting each other for control.

During the hippie era in the 1950s, 60s, and 70s, with the rejection of "the system," people advocated for free love and stuck daisies in gun barrels. Cooperative communes sprouted like mushrooms around the country. Rejection of any hierarchy was the flavor of the month. However, there were still leaders, people the others looked to for answers to complex problems.

The leaders of these communes may have rejected or pretended to reject the typical trappings of leadership, but they and their fellow commune dwellers knew the truth. The survival of the commune depended on the wisdom and decisions of their leaders and on people willing to accept and follow their visions and decisions.

Any social structure, the military, educational institutions, private enterprise, and religions all rely on this hierarchical model to maintain a sense of order. And, while most hierarchies have rules and regulations meant to maintain control, often with the threat of reprisal for those who color outside the lines, it all still requires concession or acquiescence by the ruled classes. If those down in the organization chart, which generally far outnumber those at the top, decide they're fed up with the decisions of the ruling class, you have the ingredients for a revolution, which we have seen time and time again in history.

So, the notion of superior individuals and leaders must have been one of the first realizations of early humans. Some people were bigger, stronger, or more intelligent than others. Perhaps, after we had fought and scrapped like a pack of wild dogs until we were homeless, hungry, and more than a few of us injured or dead, we concluded we needed this hierarchical society, a way to establish order to survive.

Accepting that certain individuals were stronger and wiser can, without much imagination, be translated into a theory of gods, especially if the rulers agree with that notion.

Gods who threw great bolts of lightning from the clouds controlled how much rain fell and dictated whether crops would survive. They were a force to be reckoned with. They controlled who was sick and who wasn't, who would bear children, and ultimately, they controlled the life and death of humans, at least in the minds of humans. These were all events that were a total mystery to people long ago.

When nature unleashed its fury on early humans, and since these forces were many times stronger than their mightiest warrior, leaving them as helpless as newborn babes, it was a natural progression to believe there was an even stronger force, an even mightier warrior that no one could see, who was wreaking havoc on the world. Gods, like the Norse God Loki, were prevalent in many civilizations.

Our world, our knowledge, and our imagination were so limited back then that we envisioned these gods to look like our mightiest warriors, only bigger and stronger. Thus, most of the gods took human form because we were incapable of conceiving anything else. Hand them a tool of their calling, a hammer, bolt of electricity, or a hoe, and wha-la', welcome the God of thunder, lightning, rain, fertility, harvest, and any other event beyond our comprehension.

In some cultures, the gods took the form of animals and even crops like corn. The animals that the people observed, respected, and possibly feared served humans by being or providing food, and beasts of burden became part of their religion and their gods.

Could the assignment of human form to the ancient gods explain the modern perception that man is created in God's image? Suppose we began with multiple gods. We could only conceive them as looking like us. Our intellect couldn't conjure up images of little green men. In that case, it is a straight line of natural progression, or evolution, to a single god that would also look like us, or we - like Him - because that is the way He wanted it, at least in the mind of humans. That logical path is more accessible than conjuring up some non-human form or entity to represent our God. We saved that for his adversary, the Devil.

One of the biases of the human mind that I find fascinating is that we detest a knowledge gap or void in our understanding of our world. We can't accept that something might happen for no reason. Without an understanding of why something happened, we can become quite paranoid. We want an explanation, a reason for all the things that occur in our lives. We cannot accept that we might live in a world where random events can determine the paths of our lives or our deaths. There must be a reason, a plan, or someone responsible.

Life is random but somewhat predictable, using just a bit of logic. We will use the example of someone living in a major city in the world. Although I refer to the United States, this example can be applied anywhere in the world, substituting another animal for the buffalo in some cases.

Suppose you live in New York, Chicago, Seattle, or Los Angeles. In that case, the odds of you being injured or dying in an automobile accident go way up over someone living in Wyoming, where the population of the entire state is about 7% of what it is in New York City (563,000 vs 8,400,000). With an estimated 30% of the people of New York commuting to work in their cars, individually in many urban areas, that puts 2.5 million vehicles on the road every day, or five times as many cars as there are people in the entire state of Wyoming. Therefore, more people die in automobile accidents in New York than in Wyoming.

On the other hand, the chances of being trampled by a buffalo go way up in Wyoming, where there are some 3,000 buffalo, compared to New York City, where I'm reasonably confident there are none, or at best, very few behind substantial barriers in zoos.

Your odds of being struck by lightning are much higher if you are outside and away from large structures than if you're in a building in a major city. This isn't a mystery; it is simple science, logic, and the laws of probability.

My point here is that life is random - It's random as all hell. God didn't decide to have you go to Wyoming and be trampled by a buffalo, or to be run over by a crazy cab driver in New York.

If you fear stampeding buffalo, you can take steps to minimize the possibility of your fears coming true. If large cities with a lot of traffic are your worst nightmare, you have choices. This has nothing to do with a higher power deciding if you live or die; it's a matter of chance, knowledge, personal choice, and placement.

As I read this paragraph, next to my Bloody Mary - no ice, it is possible, though a remote chance, that when I next step outside, a block of blue ice, the accidentally released bathroom waste from a passing aircraft high overhead in Seattle, could fall on me and kill me. That is a random event, not one that was planned. Nothing anyone can say will convince me that it was an orchestrated event by the God of blue ice, or any other god who is controlling the lives of over eight billion people on this planet, no matter how angry that God might be that I am an atheist and reading this book to you.

There was another reason why our ancestors imagined that the gods were controlling what was happening in their lives. It served to dispel their fears, to a degree, and put something, anything, in that knowledge gap in their thought processes. Nature abhors a vacuum, and the human brain detests a lack of answers.

By attributing the unexplainable to the gods, they had an explanation for the unknown, a kind of knowledge of the unfathomable that allowed them to get on with their lives. They could spend their time designing new tools, pondering their societal values and behaviors, looking for improvement, and complaining about their leaders, all the things most of us do daily. The theory of gods was just as mysterious as the events themselves, but at least they had a presumed authority running the show, which allowed them to pursue evolution. This evolution led us from those caves to the great cities we have today.

Well done, humans! We now had all these gods whom we could thank, or blame if you prefer, for life's mysteries. Since much of what happens in life can often be relatively unpleasant, we decided the gods must be angry at us when things went down the dumper, and we sought ways to appease them for whatever it was we must have done wrong.

Quite naturally, we assigned human traits to our gods. Since they looked like us, they must indulge in life's pleasures, eating, drinking, and making love, just like us. At some point, and it would be impossible to identify when or with whom it all began, people began to see that they could establish themselves in the clan hierarchy by becoming the subject-matter experts on the gods and all things mysterious.

Becoming a "religious" leader fed large human egos that were hungry for acceptance, power, or even adoration, and I believe it continues to serve that purpose today for many people.

Being a religious leader established prominence within the clan where none had existed, often increasing the wealth and prestige of the recipient of this presumed knowledge, knowledge of events that the average person struggled to comprehend.

Ritualistic behavior has taken many forms in different cultures throughout human history. One of the most common practices was that of sacrifice, most often animals like sheep and goats, but in some instances, human sacrifice was the norm. Again, there seems to me to be a logic to their behavior, albeit archaic, and to this practice of sacrifice as viewed from the standpoint of these ancient and frightened people, many of whom were incapable of all but limited logical thought as measured by modern standards.

A remark about that last sentence. Logic, like time, is relevant. One source defines logic as "a particular mode of reasoning viewed as valid or faulty."

I would append that definition to add "for the time." Logic must be evaluated within the context of time and the collective knowledge of that time.

What we view as valid and logical today, such as the earth's roundness and its rotation around the sun, is very different from what was viewed as valid and logical several thousand years ago when the world was believed to be flat, and the universe revolved around us. Context and time dictate what is logical and what is not.

Considering that life back then was quite challenging and the search for food an arduous and often dangerous prospect, our ancient ancestors valued a goat or sheep very highly. Your worth was frequently measured by how many goats you owned, and it remains so in some remote parts of the world today.

These animals produced milk for your family and offspring to ensure a continuation of the food supply. Occasionally, one of the animals sacrificed its life to feed us during celebrations. This was no small donation in the minds of the clan, with the owner of the animal being highly praised by the tribe for making such a sacrifice for the good of the whole.

It would make sense to these people that if they sacrificed one of their prized goats or pigs to a pissed-off god, it should be evident to this God that the people were serious in their devotion to them and hoped that such sacrifice might appease these angry gods. In turn, God would relieve whatever pain was being inflicted on the people's lives. Why else would they willingly give up their scarce and hard-fought food supply?

It is as easy as connecting the dots.

(a) The gods looked like humans.

(b) They must have the same appetites as humans.

(c) They exhibit the same emotions as humans, such as anger, boredom, etc.

(d) Therefore, the gods will appreciate the gift or sacrifice of a lamb or goat the same way any human would appreciate such a gift.

None of this mystical thinking altered the natural occurrences of nature and the roulette wheel of life that was the decider of events. Any correlation between sacrifice and the cessation of pain was purely coincidental.

Still, between their fears and their natural superstitions, all reinforced by the pontifications of their shamans or spiritual leaders, they remained convinced that sacrifices helped. Like the player on a Super Bowl-winning team, they found a way to convince themselves that when things went their way, it was because of their gods. To my way of thinking, it's like using astrology to forecast your life. When it is correct, you can point to it and insist that it is a valid belief. When it misses the mark, like our favorite team losing a game, we tend to attribute that outcome to other factors rather than to indict our belief system.

When things really went south, our ancestors reached for new solutions. The ancients were an older version of us at a much earlier time with a bit more body hair but no less inventive. It was presumed that if we sacrificed one of our fellow humans instead of a goat or sheep, a member of our beloved family of humans, the gods would have to be even more impressed by our commitment to their happiness.

Naturally, this had no more effect on the outcome of events than serving up a lamb or goat. Still, like people today, when something doesn't work, we tend to do that same thing over and over again but with a great deal more enthusiasm in the hope that we will achieve a better outcome. When a change in events occurs right after we have sacrificed or prayed, we make the connection and say, "See, it worked!" When it doesn't work out, we shrug and move on.

Early humans had little more to work with than their evolved animalistic instincts, bolstered by an evolving brain that still needed to contain a great deal of knowledge. While terribly complicated and still somewhat of a theory, the development of the frontal lobe in the human brain a few hundred thousand years ago gave rise to our creativity and curiosity about the world around us. It was a combination of instinct, fear, and an emerging brain and intellect that gave birth to religion.

Science, mathematics, or any of today's accepted academic pursuits had not yet blossomed. Coupled with what must have been a life of almost constant fear, deprivation, near starvation, hardship, fear of becoming prey to large animals, and fear of natural disasters, not to mention the fear of death, which had to be baffling to everyone, the desire to believe in the mysticism of a god, or gods, and the existence of something beyond death had to have been enticing indeed.

Many events and emotions are acting on people today, and the same was true thousands of years ago. Every generation throughout history has believed the previous generation had a more straightforward and, therefore, better and easier life. We believe there weren't as many complications in past generations as we are experiencing in our lifetime.

I disagree. Life was different, but the problems of each generation were just as difficult for them to grapple with as those of the previous or subsequent generations. We could have dealt with space travel in the eighteenth century, but because it was not yet reality, there was no need to exercise that part of our brain. It is all a matter of context.

If there was a pack of wolves howling outside your cave, and all you had was a pointy stick to ward them off, that had to be every bit as frightening as it would be today if someone with an assault weapon is breaking into your house when you are home and all you had to defend yourself with was a stick.

As we developed better tools and technology, the old problems became simpler to solve. At the same time, all of our new technology and continuing expansion as a species presented new problems that seemed far more difficult to resolve than the old ones.

Humans are persistent in their efforts to manage society and the world around them. Governments came and went, both good and bad. Laws were enacted, laws that made perfect sense to the men who penned them at the time (sorry for blaming men again, but it's true). As new generations entered the mix, many of those laws were amended or dropped altogether. This is all part of human social evolution.

Various leaders, over time, sought to get the masses to conform to a particular model of behavior and a way of thinking they believed would yield a better society. That remains the goal of leaders today, whether liberal or conservative, democratic or autocratic. We'll leave the manic elements of leadership for another day and another discussion.

The debates that rage between conservatives and progressives are a matter of how you define the model of behavior you personally embrace, your morals, and your beliefs. The tug-of-war between autocratic and democratic rule has gone on for millennia, with both camps convinced that only their approach will prevail and succeed.

But humans, being human, with our inquisitive brains and what we call free will, have never really walked lockstep through life as those in control might have preferred.

In addition to the constant chaos of changing leadership, one leader espousing one philosophy and another the opposite, as well as those claiming they were themselves indeed gods, the populace was often confused. Still, we are problem solvers, if nothing else.

Much to the dismay of these shepherds of what they hoped were mindless sheep, people were learning about the world around them. They were growing intellectually and questioning the decisions of their leaders. Leaders don't like that nor react well to their self-proclaimed wisdom being challenged. Leaders in the U.S. still haven't learned that in a nation of 330 million people, that's a lot of creative brain power questioning your every move as a leader. In a country like China, which has a billion people, the problems of leadership are tripled.

A quick aside. For centuries, China has pursued an autocratic approach to governance. From ruthless Emperors to Xi Jinping and his brand of communism combined with materialism and enforced through militaristic rule, it is the authoritarian experiment that is comparable to our democratic experiment in the United States.

The problems of governing have been the same throughout history. You can try to rule by force, but the truth is that even with all your armies, you are typically outnumbered by at least two or three hundred to one. At the end of 2013, there were 1.4 million people on active duty in the United States and about 330 million people in the country. That produces a ratio of about 237 civilians for each person in the military.

If that were not the case and everyone was in the military, you wouldn't have a country to run. There would only be you and your military. Leaders need other ways to quell the masses that have the power to bring down their government.

You could swell the ranks of your military and police by using inscription to build a mighty army. The problem with that approach is that you would be employing the very people who might disagree with you and start a coup.

You are training them in the arts of battle that they may use against you if they revolt someday. You may be polluting the loyalty of your army by forcing these miscreants to serve where they can begin to sway the minds of your faithful followers, diluting your philosophy. The odds of a coup can go way up in a situation like that.

It should seem logical to some of these leaders, those who felt the need to control the actions of others, which appears to be the norm for most people in or striving for a position of authority, that something more than military might is needed to soothe the restless citizenry.

As the multiple gods' approach was losing appeal in light of the transgressions of these gods, both human and mythological, why not a single, all-knowing, all-seeing entity that no one could claim as a relative?

Another factor that came into play is our growing intellect. While we still didn't understand how weather patterns changed or where the various elements of weather came from, some people must have started putting one and one together.

They may have observed that the wind was stronger and from different directions than normal before and just after a big storm. A sudden drop in temperature often preceded snow. Were all these gods, like wind, rain, and thunder, who had been assigned a role in all that we found mysterious, working together to create these events, or was there another explanation?

The single god theory also involved various heads of state claiming some sort of divine lineage that gave them immunity to the laws of man. After incestuous relationships and all manner of ungodly behavior proved to be a testament to not only their humanness but also their perjury, the masses looked elsewhere for their divinity. Some royal families in Europe clung to the notion of divinity for a very long time, but eventually, that fizzled out.

The leaders' sordid behavior may also have contributed to dismissing the old gods. If the gods condoned the actions of these debauched leaders, then they were a sorry excuse for a god.

A Single God

During the infancy of the monotheistic religious theory, it must have seemed obvious to those promoting this philosophy that a single God, whether benevolent or threatening, was probably not going to be enough to reign in humans' desires and misdeeds; something more was needed. At this point in human history, we have been toying with various spiritual and religious concepts for at least 45,000 years; that's a lot of history to overcome.

Most of the deliberations on how ancient people approached resolving the problem of humans behaving like primates are suppositions on my part. Remember that the first of the monotheistic leaders was Akhenaten, to the best of our knowledge, some 1,500 years before the birth of Jesus. Unquestionably, old Akhenaten didn't develop this idea on his own. There must have been people who were disaffected by the current religious practices and the behavior of humans and who had been talking this way for some time.

It is difficult, if not impossible, to know precisely what was in the minds and hearts of these early monotheists. Was their thinking an evolutionary journey, or did they have an ah-ha moment? I suspect they were distraught by the society of the day. They saw rampant corruption, men using religion for personal gain, and an abundance of debauchery. I suspect it was a gradual progression based on frustration.

If the logic of behaving civilly wasn't working, even with all the various gods to strike fear into people, then perhaps one mighty, all-powerful God might do the trick. The actual beginnings of religion, as we think of it, are lost to history due to the absence of documentation of what people were talking about five thousand and more years ago.

We have some tablets and mostly crude paintings on walls, but we can't know how the debates and conversations took place in the public squares over tea or whatever they drank back then as humans sought answers to life. Based on the eventual outcome, we can only surmise what those motivations and conversations contained.

The universe for the ancients consisted of three realms: the sky (the heavens), earth (humans), and the underworld (sometimes called the netherworld or the land of the dead). The sky was the domain of the gods and was crowded with a host of divinities understood in a gradient of powers. Many ancient civilizations had a dominant god, or a king of the gods, with other divinities overseeing various aspects of life, serving as a court of advisers, or simply as messengers to humans below.

A quick note about this concept of the underworld or netherworld. If we humans decided that there was an underworld that was generally considered a scary place, then why the hell did we decide to bury our dead in the ground? Some civilizations, like the Native Americans, seemed to understand that. The Native American cultures honored their departed with rituals deeply rooted in their spiritual connection to the natural world. These ceremonies serve as a bridge between life and the afterlife, guiding the deceased on their final journey with respect and reverence.

Not all Native American cultures elevated the dead. Some Plains Indians placed their dead on scaffolds or in trees, while others buried them. If the ground was frozen, they might have no choice but to bury them elevated. This would allow friends and relatives to visit. One would think that ritual would have been more prevalent than sticking people in the ground. Back to our discussion.

Ancient Judaism continues to receive the most attention as creating the origins of monotheism in the Western tradition. Like their neighbors, ancient Jews conceived of a hierarchy of powers in heaven: "sons of god," angels, and archangels.

Somewhere along the line, our current God, the same one that many, if not most, western religions embrace today, became an angry, jealous, and frankly, at times homicidal God. That would be the God that we read about in the Old Testament.

This single God had to be an amalgamation of all those other gods, the angry one that threw lightning bolts and the good ones who brought the spring rains that made crops go. So we came up with this good God, who, if you followed the rules which, coincidentally, were created by men, then life should be just peachy. But, if you screw up, then the angry side of God would smite you.

Those advocating for this angry God must have hoped that the fear of His wrath would be enough to get everyone to abandon their pagan celebrations, come to services, and march in a straight line. It may not have worked all that well back then, and it doesn't work that well today. But humans are persistent, if nothing else, so religions continue to seek ways to bring the masses to heel.

There is no shortage of those who talk a good game when it comes to religious and moral values, but damn few who follow through and live the life they demand that others live. I suppose that sounds a little like some of the bible-thumping conservatives who are constantly being caught with their pants down today. It is because the human tendency to engage in debauchery has proven to be a universal truth, not just for Christians but all religions, and a chronic problem for religion in general. One has to wonder if faith is antithetical to the nature of humans.

After a couple of thousand years of peddling this almighty deity, mostly by the Jews, along came a man named Jesus, a Jew, who turned out to be something of a social progressive for his time. He was dissatisfied with the conduct of the Rabbis leading the Jewish faith, of which he had been a member all his life, as well as the oppressive Roman rulers. Both institutions leaned on oppression and retribution to control the masses.

Jesus began preaching a very different philosophy of love, of helping the least among us, rejecting the ruling class with statements attributed to him about it being easier for a camel to pass through the eye of a needle than for a rich man to attain the kingdom of heaven. His teachings suggested that by following his philosophy, you were more or less promised a front-row seat in heaven with His father, or so the tale is told.

If we can believe the story of Jesus entering the temple and throwing out the money changers, Jesus was, in effect, rejecting the rabbis who were not only reluctantly allied with the Roman rulers but were themselves corrupt. Greed and riches are yet another bump in the road to eternal bliss.

It is not too much of a stretch to believe that Jesus, wanting to usurp the power of the Rabbis who served an angry God, might have been motivated to tell the people who would listen to him about a different, more benevolent God. Whether Jesus declared himself the son of God or his followers anointed him as such, the effect was to make his word indisputable in the minds of his followers and antagonize the rabbis and the Romans. His basic message, if we're to believe all that was written decades and centuries after his death, was one of peace, love, and acceptance.

If he was the Son of God, how could any other rabbi - Jesus was also a rabbi or teacher - know more about God than his son? Of course, the traditional rabbis denounced Jesus as the Messiah. They had already decreed that only they would know when the real Messiah would appear, and Jesus had not sought their permission to be that Messiah. He was about to unravel their world; he must be denounced. And denounce him they did.

After centuries of religious work and evolution to separate humans from the gods, along comes this upstart son of a carpenter from a family with no social standing, claiming, or so it is written, to be the son of God. And how was this man different from the emperors who claimed to be descendants of the gods and then behaved badly - although there is no suggestion that Jesus behaved badly? There are rumors about prostitutes and the like, but like the whole of most religions, it seems to be lore as opposed to fact. Some of the people back then must have asked all these questions.

Given that Jesus was opposed to much of what the rabbis were up to, it should surprise no one that both the Jewish leadership and Roman government would reject him, and his followers claim that he was the Messiah the Jews had been waiting for all those centuries.

To the religious rulers of the time, this was a rabble-rouser and miscreant bent on destroying their comfortable arrangement with the Roman Empire; isn't that the basis of most revolutions? To the Roman Empire, he was a radical, stirring up the masses with his off-the-wall ideas. He was a threat to their rule and stability. He had to go, and of course, in the end, he did.

Why, in an era that has seen humanity make advances such as humans walking on the moon, space vehicles soaring out into the universe, humans living for a year at a time on a space station, the invention of computers, and all the knowledge that science has brought us in the last 500 years - why do so many people not on drugs or delusional, continue to cling to this notion of an all-powerful entity that no one has ever seen, or ever heard from? And why do they follow leaders of religion who profess to have engaged in a conversation with either God or Jesus?

Why are some people so zealous that it leads them to commit horrendous acts of violence against innocent people not of their faith? If I knew the answer to that, I'd write a book — oh, wait, I did that, and I'm reading it now. Nevertheless, I do frequently question why we continue to behave, in many ways, like those poor souls five or ten thousand years ago.

I have and will continue using the term fear to the point that some of you may want to puke. I am not apologizing. We humans are fearful animals. The ultimate fear we all live with and try to ignore is death. No one knows precisely what happens after we die or when that might happen - I have my own ideas about that and will get into that further on. The only organizations to venture a guess have been various religious orders. We have been offered heaven, Nirvana, reincarnation, life on another planet, and who knows what else. Come one, come all, and drink the Kool-Aid.

As an Atheist, all I have to offer is nothing, which is what I believe follows death. I can't prove there is nothing after, any more than your chosen faith can prove the opposite. I believe we share the same fate as every other living thing on this planet: dogs, cats, rhinos, roses, or tulips. Whatever happens to all those living organisms will happen to each of us. That thought likely scares the bejesus out of many people.

Here's a short detour into the afterlife. I have an answer to what happens that suits me just fine. It may not set well with everyone, but here it is. I'm a product of what went on in my mother's womb. Once that egg was fertilized, the process that would eventually produce a small human began.

You have to understand that I don't believe we are a person for a long time into that gestation process, not until we have a functioning brain and all our organs. Until they can lay you out on a table, and you can breathe, eat, and poop on your own, you are not a viable human being. Until a little chicken pecks its way out of the shell, it's an egg on its way to being a chicken. Pop it out of the shell before it's ready, and it will die.

Okay, so I make it to at least 24 weeks of gestation, and I'm born. During that gestation period, I was the product of all the sustenance my mother provided while I was snug inside her. Everything she drank, ate, and breathed in the world around her became part of me.

One day, when I check out, I'll either be cremated or, if I can convince Gale, composted under a tree. I will now go on the journey that every living thing on this planet takes: plant, human, or animal. The essence of what I am, the gasses, the minerals, and any other elements that made my life possible, will return to the universe's cycle of life and be absorbed by another form of burgeoning life. In that way, I will live on. I won't know it, and I'm not going to join anyone, animal or human, in the afterlife. It's the giant recycling program of life.

Now, back to our discussion of religion and gods. A little more about that fear of death. Most of us have probably known people who went through life attending church only when someone close to them was either married or buried. They may have lived that way for sixty or more years, perhaps partying their asses off and violating every tenet of their sworn religion.

As they entered that twilight phase of their lives where death is much closer than their birth—that could be anywhere from fifty to seventy years of age, depending on their state of mind and health—and knowing that the curtain could come down at any time and that the end is much closer than the beginning, many people began to hedge their bets. What if there really is a heaven and a God?

No one wants to risk scuffing the toe of their shoe in cloud dust, trying to explain to Saint Peter, or the man Himself, why they spent their years on Earth ignoring Him and his creation, or worse, pooh-poohing the notion that He exists while cheating their way through life. In the end, they get serious about their religion and try to make up for the years that they turned a deaf ear to The Message, just in case. It's like buying an insurance policy for life eternal.

This offers us the opportunity to look at a timeline taking us back to around 3,000 BCE, or roughly 5,000 years into the past. I mentioned earlier that this one-God thinking might reach back as far as 50,000 years, even though this timeline only covers the last 3,000 years or so because older records do not exist.

Using a 50,000-year timeline and a 25-year generational calculation, we may have practiced this thinking for 2,000 generations. If 50,000 years of thinking, believing, and behaving based on fear and the belief in supernatural powers aren't enough to rewire the human brain (evolution of thought), then the entire idea of evolution is knocked into a cocked hat.

Practice makes perfect, and we have perfected the art of believing in the unknown, the unprovable, and the notion that some greater force is controlling our lives. It bears a striking resemblance to modern politics.

Most of us don't take the time to understand all the issues in the world. The world is a complex and, yes, a frightening place at times. We don't particularly want to confront the problems or deal with all the crap on a day-to-day basis, and we sure as hell don't want to be responsible for solving all these problems.

We elect men and women to positions in government who will tell us what is going on. We want them to say to us that all is well or will be after they work their magic that they have assured us during campaign speeches will protect us from harm. They are, if you will, the ministers, priests, and imams of civil law.

We want to go our merry way, engaged in whatever pleasures of the mind and body amuse us currently, and let others worry about the future. Science, roughly 500 years old and as advanced as it has become, has a tough row to hoe against 50,000 years of mystical conditioning.

Religion provides the salve for our conscience and our psychological well-being. It can forgive us our sins, which are in the triple digits for most of us who have been trundling around this planet for at least twenty years. And our church leaders keep telling us to relax; it will all be okay in the end.

Depending on your religion, you have a number of purging opportunities for your sins. You can confess your sins, fast for some time, go on pilgrimages, and in severe cases, flog yourself with a whip laced with sharp objects (or perhaps whip others) until you bleed, or stone offenders to death, or hang them in the public square. We are told that by doing so, we, or the unfortunate sinner, can be washed clean of our sins and, more importantly, be assured of eternal life in some beatific great beyond.

How the hell did the concept of self-inflicted pain, killing, and even mutilation become linked with piety and morality? Oh, that's right, the thorns, hauling the cross up the hill, that sort of thing. And let's not forget the Old Testament and an eye for an eye; good old Leviticus is full of rationale for killing offenders. There are some real sadists in this world.

But consider the reward if you follow the word. Who can resist the promise of life everlasting in a place where all is love and peace? Who can resist a promise of a harem of seventy-two virgins? That, by the way, is a distorted myth of what Islam offers. The exact quote goes like this, "We have created mates for them and made them virgins, matched in age, for the companions of the right hand." (56:35-38). Sure, that is a little sexist, but you have to remember that most of this was designed by men; what do you suppose was on their minds when they penned this gem?

The number 76, or 72, or any other number has nothing to do with Islam. Much like the promises of Christianity, Islam promises, well, a different version of heaven. Apparently, the founders of Islam place great importance on their women being virgins. Nevertheless, I find this a strange thing to promise in the name of religion.

A quick note about the term virgin: a debate rages about the word virgin and its application to the birth mother of Jesus, Mary. There is a strong argument that virgin, from the Latin Virgo, originally meant a young woman. It has little or nothing to do with abstaining from sex. The authors of the Christian texts redefined the word to suggest an immaculate conception that produced Jesus. The New Testament is relatively silent on the virgin birth except in two places. It appears only in the gospels of Matthew and Luke, written a few decades after Jesus' death.

Back to our discussion of religion and our behavior. If we go astray as most humans will do and seem at times almost compelled to do, we repeat our repentant process to emerge clean once again, feeling assured we will live in eternal bliss. If we fall again and get dirty, we take another theological shower.

For all our technological advances and our exponentially increasing intellect, there is something in our reptilian brain that wants to be free of fear and doubt; fear of death, doubt about the future, and with an understanding that all that happens in our lives is part of some grand plan, and of course, the assurance that there is something after our death.

The notion that this life is all there is - not only scares the crap out of us, but it scares the crap out of our leaders. If none of us believed there was anything after this life, if we didn't think we would live in a burning hell for eternity for our sins, why would we care what a politician, cop, judge, teacher, priest, preacher, Rabbi, or imam had to say about how we lived our lives? We would party our asses off for eighty years if our bodies would hold out and die happy if there is nothing beyond this.

Why would we resist our self-serving, animalistic urges? If there is no punishment for doing bad things and no reward for being a good citizen, employee, neighbor, husband or wife, father or mother, what kind of world would this be? If we're all going to end up worm food, why not party to the end?

Maybe there's another approach that doesn't threaten us with spending eternity in a damn cremation oven. Guess who, in my opinion, seems to have this part of the puzzle of life figured out? Or at least are perhaps the closest to the answer of an orderly society that I know of without the threat of damnation, flogging, stoning, or the severing of selected limbs?

The Buddhists, and most likely many of the Native American tribes, and perhaps other Indigenous people around the world that I'm not aware of or that I haven't taken the time to explore – many of them seem to have arrived at a similar conclusion.

Almost everyone has spent some time on Earth trying to understand who we are and why we are here. And, just as I believe the origins of Christianity have been warped over time by the self-serving interpretations of egotistical people (AKA perverted evolution), so I think the teachings of all the other philosophies have suffered the same sort of revisionism.

When you look at Buddhism's basic tenets, you will generally find that its teachings are more philosophy than religion because there is no omnipotent being that you are supposed to bow down to or be afraid of. It is pretty straightforward.

- Lead a moral life - okay, you have to define morals, but we can probably reach a consensus on that.

- Be mindful and aware of your thoughts and actions and how they impact others and the world we live in - that doesn't need a lot of interpretation or explanation.

- Develop wisdom and understanding—eh, this is another one where we might need to define what we mean by wisdom, but that should be doable.

It's pretty damned difficult to argue with any of those three guiding principles, and they are a heck of a lot easier to remember and follow than the ten commandments and a slew of contradictory verses from a book stitched together by a bunch of older men. Another plus, you don't need a heavy stone tablet to carry around with all this chiseled on the face.

Buddhism is based on four truths.

1. The first truth is that life is suffering, i.e., life includes pain, getting old, disease, and ultimately death. We also endure psychological suffering like loneliness, frustration, fear, embarrassment, disappointment, and anger. This is an irrefutable fact that cannot be denied. The hippies of the 60s

summed it up when they said, "Shit happens, and then you die." It is realistic rather than pessimistic because pessimism expects things to be bad. Instead, Buddhism explains how suffering might be avoided and how we can be truly happy. That's different from many religions that tell us we have to suffer all our lives and that it's the price we pay to get to heaven.

2. The second truth is that suffering is caused by craving and aversion. We will suffer if we expect other people to conform to our expectations, if we want others to like us, if we do not get something we want, etc. In other words, getting what you want does not guarantee happiness. Try to modify your wants rather than constantly struggling to get what you want. Wanting deprives us of contentment and happiness. A lifetime of wanting and craving, and especially the craving to continue to exist, creates a powerful energy that causes the individual to be born. So, craving leads to physical suffering because it causes us to be reborn.

I would add another point to this truth: expectations. We develop expectations, sometimes unrealistically, and then we are unhappy when those expectations aren't met. It's normal to have expectations, but we need to keep them real. I love to use this in connection with dining out. We love Italian food, and Gale especially loves a Puttanesca sauce with pasta. We go to a new restaurant that has the sauce on the menu. We know what we like and what we expect, and if they don't meet our expectations, we're upset.

The truth might be that the sauce they make is excellent, but because we provided a very narrow definition of good, the restaurant was doomed to failure, and we were doomed to be disappointed. A little less rigidity in our expectations can ease a lot of suffering. Obviously, that's a relative thing. We expect our doctors to know what they're doing, and they should. Ranking your expectations based on quality of life could be helpful. A good doctor is critical. A perfect Puttanesca is not.

3. The third truth is that suffering can be overcome, happiness can be attained, and true happiness and contentment are possible. If we give up useless cravings and learn to live each day one day at a time (not dwelling in the past or the imagined future), then we can become happy and free. We then have more time and energy to help others. This is described as Nirvana.

4. The fourth truth is that the Noble Eightfold Path leads to the end of suffering. In summary, the Noble Eightfold Path involves being moral (through what we say, do, and our livelihood), focusing the mind on being fully aware of our thoughts and actions, and developing wisdom by understanding the Four Noble Truths and compassion for others.

No, I am not a Buddhist, and I'm not trying to convert anyone to Buddhism or any other philosophy. I am trying to point out that it is possible to follow common-sense teachings about a peaceful world that doesn't depend on fear of some angry omnipotent being, expulsion from a church or society, or a life in a burning hell.

It would be tough for anyone to refute the tenets of what preceded this paragraph as a life philosophy and one that would make this world a much more peaceful place to live. I should explain that I find the reincarnation concept of Buddhist philosophy to be as unbelievable as the heaven and hell theories and hold about the same credibility.

I also understand that trying to be pure to the four truths is borderline impossible for most of us, probably at least as hard as following the teachings of most religions.

Really? No more cravings for chocolate ice cream? I'm going to guess even Mother Theresa succumbed at times to cravings, so no one is perfect. Still, the Buddhist approach is a good way to try to live your life on a day-to-day basis.

If you take Buddhism to the extreme, you might spend all your time doing nothing. Our culture and way of life have been based on moving forward, innovation, and looking for improvement, so we need a modified version of Buddhism that allows for capitalism and even an assertive approach with boundaries regarding harming others or our environment. Okay, enough preaching.

By now, I assume I have pissed off just about every religion on the planet — well, I haven't picked on the Hindus yet, but then I am not done either.

As for the Native Americans, I think the picture of their original belief system has been muddied a bit by the invasion of and efforts by the Europeans to "civilize" the indigenous people they found on this continent; you know, the ones we called savages, on a good day.

From this point on, I will use the term Indians, both for its simplicity and to include all the indigenous people of what we now call North and South America.

A brief geography/history lesson might be in order here. North America is not just the United States. North America includes the United States, Mexico, and Canada. The Americas include all these, as well as Central America and South America. So, all you United Statesians, lose this parochial attitude that North America is only about the U.S. — that is so much bullshit.

It's time for another brief tirade. You must be used to me doing that by now. We are not the only Americans, though we in the United States seem to think that way. Everyone in this hemisphere is an American; thus, all the land mass on this side of the world is referred to as the Americas.

Call yourself a U.S. citizen, a USian, whatever name you like. How about, "I am an American from the United States, Mexico, Canada, Brazil, Chile, or Argentina?" We in the U.S. do not own the title of American. Just be happy they didn't use another discoverer's last name, Vespucci – we would all be Vespuccians.

Columbus didn't discover North America; he landed on a Caribbean island. While Columbus may have been the first European to reach Central America, Giovanni Caboto was the first to arrive in North America, landing in Labrador, off the east coast of Canada, in 1497.

Caboto was beaten to North America by 500 years by the Vikings. Definitive proof of Norse habitation of Newfoundland, near Labrador, can be found at L'Anse aux Meadows, a Viking settlement dating to around 1000 C.E. The Vikings are the earliest group to leave behind tangible evidence of their presence. But wait! There's more.

In the sixth century, St. Brendan, an Irish monk who was widely reputed as a skilled seafarer, is said to have undertaken an ambitious voyage. Brendan and a crew of fellow monks sailed looking for Paradise, the Land of Promise of the Saints. It wasn't until the ninth century that an account of Brendan's voyage surfaced, the Navigatio Sancti Brendani ("Travels of St. Brendan" in Latin). It was an instant hit, translated into several languages.

So, North Americans might be called Brendanians or Cabotoans instead of Americans. Okay, enough historical shenanigans - on with our discussion of religion.

The term Indian came to us because Columbus, while unquestionably brave in venturing across the ocean in boats smaller than some of today's moderate-sized yachts on a sea that almost everyone thought was flat and dreadfully dangerous, was a man who, besides having balls the size of an elephant, wasn't that great a navigator (he got lost). To be fair, there was no GPS or even world maps at that point.

Like most people of the time, Columbus was mostly ignorant of the world's geography, and understandably so—no one had yet seen this part of the world. Unless you accept the lore that Father Brendan of Ireland sailed in sheep—or goat-skinned canoes from the Emerald Isle to the North American continent.

Back to our lost navigator, Cristoforo. When his boat bumped into one of the Bahamian islands, most likely San Salvador, he was convinced he had reached India, his preferred destination and original quest. Columbus wasn't engaged in discovery as much as he was after easy access to spices, gold, and all that India offered.

He was met by "Indians". It was an understandable mistake since he thought he was in India; the natives were dark-skinned, and he couldn't understand their language. Thus, he called the local natives Indians. Those damn brown-skinned people all looked alike even back then.

My earlier reference to the picture of Native American beliefs (remember, that means all the Americas) having been distorted is regarding the hellbent efforts in the early days of European conquest, primarily by the Catholics but later the Protestants, generally represented by the pilgrims, to convert these so-called heathens to God and their particular spin on the Christian religion.

It is this influence that I tend to think accounts for some of what, I believe, is the warped version of the spirituality of the modern Indians, referring to the United States Indians now because I tend to think I am more familiar with our Indians than those of all the Americas.

It is time for another caveat and to reiterate my earlier point: that it is always a philosopher's prerogative. When I use the general term Indian in this section, I will be referring to the Native Americans who lived in the continental United States, also referred to as the lower forty-eight.

This is not meant to show any disrespect toward the indigenous people in Alaska or Hawaii, who certainly are part of the United States and have their own stories of how outsiders screwed with their culture. Nor is it to diminish the role of all the Indians in Mexico and Central and South America. It is only for the purpose of discussing spiritual beliefs with a degree of brevity that would not be possible if I tried to address what happened to all the indigenous people in every country on the planet.

In Indian poetry and verse, there are references to the "Great Spirit," which most of us assume is our God (because we are white and Christian). Though I have no proof, I'm pretty sure that the Indians, BWM (before white men), didn't have such a term, nor do I think they believed there was one single mighty spirit that directed all events.

On the contrary, their beliefs revolved around a great many spirits and a strong belief that they were one with the world and nature, no better and no worse than any other creature that shared the planet. There were animal spirits, sun spirits, eclipse spirits, night spirits, forest spirits, and sea spirits to name a few.

Does that sound familiar? Go back and read a little about the Buddhists, or better yet, do some research on your own about the spirituality of indigenous people worldwide.

Depending on the tribe, and you'll have to excuse my awkward pronunciation if you speak any of these languages, the Apache had

Ussen, Giver of Life; the top guy for the Blackfoot tribe was Apistotoki; for the Cherokee, it was Unetlanvhi, the Creator; and for the Navajo, Yebitsai is thought to be the head of their deities. Every tribe had a list of spirits they revered.

In my opinion, the Indian religion, which isn't as much a religion as a philosophy, is more like Buddhism. It revolves around the love and appreciation of nature and all of humanity. Nature is revered for all it has to offer humans in their well-being and their struggle to survive.

There were dances to the spirits, with people assuming the visage of animals that were part of their world, animals that contributed to their survival and success, providing food and clothing.

People were given nicknames that often revered a deed the individual had accomplished or a talent or trait they had demonstrated similar to one of the animals in their world. It was an honor to be called a bear, a raven, an eagle, etc.

When they reached puberty, young boys would go into the wilderness, where they could receive a vision of Native American spirituality that would guide them throughout their lives.

I didn't know it back then, but when I was in the Boy Scouts in Nebraska, we had a ceremony at summer camp that was based on and tried to mirror this tradition. It was called the Order of the Arrow.

Boys were singled out by scoutmasters, perhaps 10% of a troop, and at a ceremony at night, were knocked backward from a circle around a campfire, taken to the woods with a few matches and a pocket knife, where we stayed all night by ourselves. Yes, I was chosen at about age thirteen, and it scared the crap out of me.

While out there alone at night, we carved a wooden arrow from a tree branch and contemplated our navels. We imagined all the horrors in the woods and jumped at every sound until someone took us back to camp in the morning. That next day, until sundown, we were not allowed to speak. The local Indians likely found all of this rather humorous, these little white boys pretending to be Indians, but it was a big deal for us.

Girls did not go through our Order of the Arrow or any true Native American spiritual ceremony, to the best of my knowledge, but then, I'm not an expert on all the tribe's ceremonies.

To understand the "religion" of the Indians is not something you can get from a book, and certainly not from my babble, or anywhere else for that matter. You have to live the life of the Indian and be told the stories of their life and the suffering at the hands of the Europeans that have been passed down through the generations to grasp what it must be like to be an Indian and carry the pain of that history with you.

On the other hand, we can gain a degree of understanding, tolerance, and acceptance, in addition to an open mind, with a bit of research and reading into their history. We can gain respect for the beauty of the fundamental and fascinating perceptions of how humanity interacts with the world around us. We can learn a great deal from the Indians and other cultures who have devoted centuries to living on the Earth and respecting nature, the nature we seem to be hellbent on destroying. You are welcome to apply this advice about learning, understanding, and acceptance to any group of people you don't understand.

Our world today is beset with pollution, animal extinction, and natural resource depletion, and there is a fading sense of hope that we can turn this ship of life we call Earth around.

We can turn it around if we get serious about it really soon, but I don't know where the point of no return might be. No one does. Perhaps we can learn from our Indian brothers and sisters. They have much more experience living with and tending to nature than most of us. While the Europeans cum Americans were hellbent on finding gold, killing buffalo, and converting indigenous people to Christianity, the Indians were trying to preserve their way of life and the nature they so loved. Maybe an Indian president, or at least someone in the president's cabinet to guide our efforts, could bear some fruit. Why not a Native American at the head of the EPA?

Not too long ago (it's 2024 as I speak), the Biden administration nominated, and the Senate confirmed Ms. Deb Haaland as Interior Secretary by a vote of 51 to 40, making her the first Native cabinet secretary in US history. Man, for a country claiming to be the greatest democracy in history, it certainly takes us a long time to do the right thing.

My reason for delving into these two non-religious religions, Buddhists and Native Americans, neither of which rely on houses of worship or require Pope-like characters to rule over all the followers of one belief or another, is to demonstrate that societies can exist in peace, and prosper without the threat of an almighty being who, on the day of judgment, will send some to heaven and others to an eternal burning hell. Seriously, folks, what a horrible choice and concept.

This is not to put the Indian or Buddhist societies on some pedestal. They were and remain far from perfect societies, as are those ruled by "traditional" religions. An ideal society does not exist, and I doubt it ever will exist because we are humans, but we can strive to be much better than we are.

The samurai of Japan, Buddhist as far as I know, were some of the fiercest and, at times, most brutal warriors in history, who hired out to the highest bidder, typically wealthy landowners who had turned their back on the local government and formed armies of their own.

In a word, the samurai were mercenaries with no particular loyalty or affiliation except to money, and yet they were Buddhists.

In the Far East, there are militant Buddhist sects who have committed horrible ethnic atrocities, most likely in the belief their cause is justified, but acts that nevertheless fly in the face of what I understand to be the philosophy of Buddhism.

I've discussed Native Americans, but they were often at war with other Indian nations. Some tribes sought peace and harmony, while others raided, stole from, and killed other tribes and enslaved people, all while embracing the same basic philosophy about nature.

The world is not perfect, and the pursuit of perfection is a recipe for misery and a fool's folly. Striving for improvement in the direction of perfection is a noble pursuit, but perfection is not attainable. Common sense and logic will reap greater rewards than all the dogma in the world.

I could go on for hours (and it may seem that I already have) citing examples like this, but dear listener, I'll give you a break from my blather and move on.

All of this contemplation, I suspect, still leaves the question of "why religion" lingering in the listener's mind. That is not an easy question, nor are there any easy answers. I am sometimes bewildered that in an age that has accomplished so much, curing disease, traveling in space, and much of the world walking around with a computer called a smartphone in their purse or back pocket, a device that would have filled a large room only 60 years ago, that so many people continue to hang on to this ancient notion of a supreme being pulling the strings that determine who lives and dies, and how they die, and pretty much everything else in the universe.

We are asked to believe in a God who orchestrates the formation and disintegration of stars, solar systems, and entire galaxies and, at the same time, directs the lives of slightly over eight billion humans living on the Earth, guiding every individual one by one.

Not only that, but we are asked to believe that he visits wars, disease, pestilence, and pain on us as a way of testing our faith. What sort of God, who is purported to be loving and forgiving, would do that?

I get it that some use religion to advance themselves. However, I think some of these people are afraid to go out into the world and compete with others for success in the corporate world or other competitive pursuits.

And some, a minority, one hopes, see it as a way to make a shitload of money from the frightened and vulnerable masses. People like Jim Jones come to mind as one of the worst, but there are others. And there are, undoubtedly, those who genuinely feel called to religion and believe they are doing the work of God. I tend to refer to that as having a Mother Teresa complex.

Regardless of their motivation for becoming religious leaders, they have a captive audience that very much wants or may need to hear what they have to say. That audience will likely cling to every word uttered from the pulpit. If the individuals in the pulpit have an ounce of personality and salesmanship, they will be lionized as great spiritual leaders. Much like an actor or singer on stage, they thrive on this admiration.

And there are, it seems to me, people who need these beliefs to cope with the travails of life. Life scares the crap out of some people, and they need to be herded, mothered, and assuaged that all will be well in the end.

For all our science, knowledge, and technological advances, we humans are still dogged by irrational fear. The fear of death trumps just about everything else in life. No one wants to die, at least no one with their head screwed on straight or who is not suffering some horrible chronic illness such as depression or incurable cancer.

Most of us don't think about death every day. What we do think about is the mortgage, the kid's dental needs, whether our job is secure, if our partner still loves us, whether the boss likes us, if our car will continue to run without breaking down —, there are a myriad of things that scare us daily. None of which that man upstairs could give a rip about, even if he did exist.

Some fears are big, some small, but collectively, they can reduce us to a quivering mass of flesh, incapable of continuing down the road of life. We need to be told that someone, somewhere, is thinking of us, looking after and protecting us.

And, if the shit does hit the fan, we can believe there is a reason our lives became a honey bucket of nasty events and that the sun will rise again tomorrow and life will be better, maybe. If it doesn't get better and all the problems hasten our end, then we are promised a better time in the afterlife, seeing all our past relatives, pets, and everyone. How can you turn down a deal like that, not just a lifetime guarantee, but one for eternity, no matter how shitty things turn out?

Then there are the tragedies that befall all of us, the monstrous life events that hang over everyone's head, threatening to turn our life into a living hell. Imagine, if you will, that you lose an infant child. How horrible must that be? How many people would lose their grip on reality under those circumstances, going off the deep end and either hurting themselves or someone else without their faith? Without being able to embrace the idea that their child isn't really dead, they would go bonkers.

To believe that your baby livs on in the presence of God has to be huge, the ultimate antidepressant when it comes to dealing with such a tragedy. Come to think of it, big Pharma must hate religion, competing with them for the mentally distressed.

What if you suffer a debilitating stroke, are diagnosed with ALS, or find yourself in a dark alley facing four armed and angry crackheads who want not only your money but a piece of your ass? How do you deal with all this? Unless you are Superman, you start by crapping your pants. If you are religious, you pray your ass off. Either way, whatever is destined to happen will happen.

If you are religious, you seek solace in the adage that "God has a plan for everyone." Your infant child is in heaven because God called your baby to Him. What a wonderful and consoling thought. Did you survive the mugging in the alley? Thank God! You go home, throw your clothes in the washer, and get on with your life, content in the belief that someone is looking after you.

That was also God's plan if you didn't survive the mugging. If you only got your ass kicked and spent a couple of months in traction, that too was God's plan. He's teaching you some lessons, though it can be difficult to see what that might be through swollen eyes.

What doesn't kill you makes you stronger. I'm pretty sure some preacher somewhere came up with that one, just in case some of the folks in his flock weren't buying his line of. . . dogma. I do know that the origin of the word dogma is from the Greek, dokein, meaning "to seem; think; seem good".

Behind every cloud is a silver lining. When one door closes, another one opens. Does that crap sound familiar? These, and any number of platitudes, are meant to soothe and appease those who have been crapped on by life. Songwriters, especially the country folks, have made a fortune playing on those euphemisms. Just tune in to the local Country Western station for a dose of how to deal with getting dumped on by your lover, boss, or trusty old pickup.

To repeat, no one wants to believe that life is random or that the turn of a wheel of fortune dictates how your life, or death, unfolds. Oh-oh, the wheel stopped on cancer or a car accident instead of winning the lottery. Tough luck, pally boy. Randomness and chance are propositions, a life philosophy most people won't consider.

So, despite all the educational, social, and technological advances humans have made, we continue to live in the dark, in places in our minds where fear, as opposed to logic, rules our behavior. Hello again to our reptilian brain.

There is a reason for this, in my opinion. It is one of the reasons that racism, discrimination, and a number of other less desirable human traits are so difficult to eradicate. We have perfected the art of both fear and discrimination and not without good reason.

There was a time, back there, when our time machine dumped us 50,000 years ago, when we needed all this fear and looked at and listened with all our built-in filters for dangers and strangers we might encounter.

Back then, with no medicine to protect us from disease, no organized police forces between us and those bent on doing us harm, no national military to protect us from the oppressions and ravages of conquering armies or batshit crazy terrorists, we needed fear. It was part of our survival technique.

We were in danger at every turn. Large animals saw us as a snack. Other tribes wanted our food, our women, and our children as indentured slaves – those would be the lucky children who only had to toil in the fields for their survival - some suffered a much worse fate.

By being wary of strangers, like a small bird feeding on the ground with its tiny head spinning about on its scrawny little neck, to avoid predators, we learned to be alert to the dangers that lurked nearby, many of them ready to end our lives. We developed a great many coping skills to survive in a world many times more threatening than anything we have to deal with today.

Social Evolution

As part of our social evolution, we honed our skills to identify potential problems and increase our ability to spot actual or possible dangers. Whether there was any foundation for those fears was immaterial. It was far better to err on the side of caution. We developed a sharp sense of fear, looking and listening to all the things we needed to be fearful of and taking defensive measures to avoid the dangers.

As those instincts applied to interacting with other tribes and clans, once we understood that other humans were only too willing to steal every damn thing we had, I believe various tribes began to adopt ways to separate themselves from others. That could be a unique mode of dress, hairstyles, body painting, and tattoos that all became a form of identification. We developed a distinctive language or dialect just for our tribe. That allowed us to converse in a way that made it difficult for outsiders to understand, separating us from other tribes as well as helping us identify outsiders. I think much of this was instinctual as opposed to a grand scheme we developed on any intellectual level.

Unlike many animals that evolved varying shapes and colors to enhance their survival, naked humans had a tendency to look much alike. Regionally, we may have developed skin color, but I think this had more to do with climate than a need to identify each other. Europe and the Mediterranean, for instance, were almost all light-skinned, and in Africa, darker skin developed due to more sun exposure.

We adopted clothes for protection from the elements and as a form of identification. If we saw someone not wearing our colors, sporting our body paint or piercings, or not speaking our language, we believed they were a potential threat to us and our loved ones.

In other words, we discriminated against people who looked or sounded different from the members of our tribe, and we did so with a genuine purpose and a high degree of expertise.

Now, assuming I'm not delusional and my premise is accurate or at least reasonably close to how we developed as a species, we lived in this dangerous world for at least fifty thousand years, probably much longer. We not only perfected the art of fear and discrimination, but we hardwired our brains to operate based on distrust.

Parents created fairy tales to scare the crap out of kids, honing their fear capabilities and preparing them for a dangerous world once they left their parents' protection.

This was all part of the process called evolution. You want things that are critical to your survival to be second nature, built into your psyche so that you don't have to stop and think about what to do next in an emergency.

When a hungry giant anaconda emerged from the bush, you needed to react to that danger without hesitation. You didn't have the time or luxury to call a meeting to discuss the best course of action, hoping everyone came to a consensus before one or more of you were on the inside and unable to look out or speak up.

Somewhere around the middle of the 19th century, although the process had been ongoing for centuries, our world became a less threatening place to live, at least for many of us. We moved into cities and became more civilized compared to the generations preceding us.

We no longer needed these instincts to survive, or at least not the same ones, or all of them, and not at the same level of intensity. The saber-toothed tiger was no more, and most of the giant wily beasts and snakes bent on turning us into their dinner had either been conquered or pushed deep into the forests, swamps, and up the mountainsides away from civilization.

Many people think science was born around 1100 and fully bloomed by the 1500s. It analyzed the world and universe around us and gave us answers to hitherto unanswered questions about our world.

People like Da Vinci, Copernicus, Hieronymus Brunschwig, Jakob Nufer, Janssen, and Galileo catapulted us from the Dark Ages into what must have seemed light years into the future.

Various societies were dallying with forms of democracy or, at minimum, developing a low tolerance for the dictatorial whims of a monarchy that was corrupt at best and often despotic.

The prospect of science explaining away much of what held us hostage to the church of our choice threatened those who made a living feasting on our fears to keep their flock together while garnering the creature comforts enjoyed by many religious leaders.

It should come as no surprise to thinking beings that religion rejected the ravings of these scientists as heretical and misguided. It is a historical fact that in the early days, the churches brought more than a few scientists up on charges of heresy, blasphemy, and even witchcraft.

Giordano Bruno was an Italian Dominican friar, philosopher, mathematician, poet, and astrologer. His cosmological theories, much celebrated, went even further than the then-novel Copernican model.

He proposed that the stars were just distant suns surrounded by their exoplanets, raising the possibility that these planets could even foster life. He insisted that the universe is, in fact, infinite and could have no celestial body at its "center."

In 1593, the smart-ass Bruno was tried for heresy by the Roman Inquisition on charges including denial of several core Catholic doctrines (including the Trinity, the divinity of Christ, the virginity of Mary, and Transubstantiation - the change by which bread and wine in the Eucharist become Christ's real presence. The Inquisition found him guilty, and in 1600, he was burned at the stake in Rome's Campo de Fiori.

Today, in a comparatively safe world for most of us, notwithstanding the gangbangers, goofball terrorists, and ever-present small percentage of bad guys, we still bend to these instinctive fears.

No matter your race or ethnic origin, when you meet a stranger from another race or country, a certain degree of discomfort rises in your chest. A stranger with an accent, possibly a tourist in our city, stops us and asks us for information. We try to be polite and helpful but cannot shake that feeling they are from somewhere else. People of color scare the crap out of most white folks, and likely, vice versa. Those ancient instincts are still protecting us from fears that, for the most part, are no longer necessary.

The difference today, and one that has been at our disposal for more than a few centuries, is that we have this marvelous brain that can be our ally. The fears that play all these mental games with us, running horror movies through our thoughts, convincing us that someone doesn't like us, or they are talking about us, are instinctive demons from the past; it happens to all of us.

We might think someone is in love with us or hates us and wants to do us harm; these are all creations in our minds. As a Mexican friend of mine, Fabiola likes to say, our mind is running movies in our head. Our brain is working overtime trying to warn and protect us from danger, dangers that, for the most part, are no longer reality.

This same brain that can make us crazy can also understand the journey we've been on for thousands of years and that the fear we are experiencing is no longer valid. This feeling is only our old reptilian brain at work, the one that served us so well in a dangerous world for tens of thousands of years, and is now causing us to feel unfounded fear.

Once we understand what is going on in our minds and why we feel the way we do, we will realize it is just a hangover from the past. We can make a conscious decision to dismiss those feelings and thoughts and get on with our lives. That person of color or with an accent is not a danger to us.

A quick anecdote at this point. This one isn't about the ancients but took place in our lives not that long ago. My wife, Gale, and I celebrated forty years of marriage in December 2014. We both love Mexico – not the Cancun or Puerto Vallarta scene, although we have been to PV, Acapulco, and up and down the West Coast and enjoyed every minute of our time there. We know these spots are popular with many people because they can "feel safe" and lounge on the beaches. You won't see us there because no one wants to see us even half-naked on the beach these days.

Our dream trip in 2014 was to the interior of Mexico to learn more about the country's history, the Mayans and Aztecs, the influence of the Spanish invaders, and other Europeans and Asians who have contributed to producing the country we know today. Yes, Asians played an important role in the eastern invasion of this side of the world.

We joked about going to see the real Mexico. Of course, all of Mexico is real, but many of the beach resorts cater to tourists, giving them what they want and not putting things like iguanas on the menu. We didn't have iguanas on our trip; they weren't offered where we were, but we would have if they had been on the menu. I did have ant eggs on a salad in Mexico City.

We booked four weeks in Mexico, starting in Merida in the Yucatán, then on to Mexico City, where we would celebrate our anniversary, Christmas, and New Year's, and then to Guadalajara for tequila, mariachis and great food (the food was great all over Mexico).

The response was nearly universal when we told friends and family what we were up to, going into the bowels of Mexico. Between the dire warnings of kidnappings, drug gangs cutting off our heads, or drug cartels stuffing balloons of cocaine up our butts, you would have thought we were off to Syria (still suffering a horrible civil war) and into the heart of territory held by ISIS, ISIL, or whatever they are called these days.

None of these horror stories came true. Here we are, safe and sound, back in Seattle, having had one of the best vacations of our lives. The people, the food, the music, the history, and the art were all fantastic.

More importantly, we walked the streets of these cities in the wee hours of the morning without fear and even a hint of a problem. We humans let our minds play devious tricks to the point of distraction. Beware those horror movies running through your mind.

The US media has done a massive disservice to the country of Mexico by scaring the doo-doo out of tourists from the United States. Sound familiar? Sounds a little like scaring the crap out of people in church with stories that threaten their peace of mind, in my opinion? But that has been both a political and religious ploy for thousands of years.

We didn't go to Mexico on a packaged tour. We asked our AAA agent to book a hotel in the center of each of the three cities we were visiting and to make sure we had airfare between the cities and then back home again. Beyond that, we would set our agenda.

For us, that meant that during the day, we would visit all the things that interested us: archeological sites, historical and art museums, some of the major tourist attractions, or sometimes walk around the cities enjoying the people, the architecture, and the culture, stopping for a leisurely lunch somewhere at the spot the locals like to frequent, and of course, shopping.

At night, we were dining, drinking, and mixing with all the Mexicans who were doing the same thing. We did not have one single problem, whether at noon or when we came back to our hotel at 2:00 a.m.

So, my advice? Ditch the fears you have about going to Mexico. Pack up and go if you love Mexican food, music, and the people. You don't want to be on your deathbed regretting that you didn't go or regretting anything that means a lot to you, no matter what it might be.

I have since told everyone who will listen that they shoot people for fun in Los Angeles. Does that stop anyone from going to Disneyland? Chicago and New York City are literal shooting galleries. Does that prevent travelers from vacationing in those cities? Do you hear the U.S. media warning you away from any of these places because of violence, which in most cases amounts to indiscriminate shooting for the fun of it and all three of these areas are at least if not more dangerous than most of Mexico?

In any city or country, there are areas that you might want to avoid - even the locals will tell you that. Still, there is no reason to avoid Mexico City, Los Angeles, Paris, Athens, or any number of marvelous vacation spots in the world. Do not be buffaloed by the fear spewed out for public consumption by corporations — yes, the media is owned by corporations — with an agenda that usually pumps money into their pockets. Depending on the media owner, they may be motivated either by getting you to watch their news program or by their larger political agenda.

Be aware that the travel and tourist industry is a multi-billion dollar enterprise. If, as happened through much of the 20th century, companies are willing to tell you that tobacco is safe in the pursuit of profits, they are not above trying to nudge you one way or another when it comes to what network you watch or how, and where you should spend your vacation money. Money and misinformation are a tangled web of deceit of the profiteers.

No, I will not apologize for getting off-topic just a little when I think a viewpoint has merit. This is tangential to my discussion of unfounded fear, so I am justified.

The same evolutionary process that led us down the path of religion to where we are today has also made us evolve from grunting animals to intellectual beings. Don't let anyone corrupt your mind, whether it's a politician, travel expert, religious leader, or the media. Do your research and use that marvelous brain to decide for yourself what is what.

Now, I will return to my theme of religious evolution. To summarize why religion came to be, the ancient humans were emerging from their earlier roots as animals, driven purely by instinct. We had evolved a larger brain that was growing larger and capable of more complex thought all the time. Still, our knowledge of what went on in our lives and our world needed to be more extensive to populate our newly evolved intellect with an understanding of our world, our solar system, and the universe. The knowledge that would, once acquired, ward off many of our old suspicions and fears.

Until we developed that knowledge, much of it based on science, our big marvelous brain had all this capacity but nothing to put there. The best we could do at that point was to fill it with stories and fairy tales spun by our society's leaders. For the most part, our reptilian brain was still informing us.

Remember me saying that nature and the human mind detest vacuums? The ancients had a serious vacuum in their brains. That void was filled with wild tales while we continued to develop our own ideas, often using simple logic, and science began to answer many of our questions.

This is another short detour concerning this large and largely empty brain we have developed. As we learned more about the world in which we lived and found ways to improve our lives on this planet, we were also freed to explore our world even more.

To explain that last statement, I will call on Carl Sagan, a man of science, a Renaissance man, and, in my opinion, a man who, in his own right, is up there with Da Vinci.

In one of his books, The Dragons of Eden, Sagan discussed the evolution of the human mind. At one point, and I'm using my best recollection at this point as opposed to reading his book again, he discussed the advent of writing and its impact on humanity.

Until that point in our development, all civilizations depended on storytellers to pass on the history of the tribe. There were no books, libraries, or Internet where we could go to discover information. We depended entirely on the storytellers, hoping they weren't distorting the facts too much.

Once we developed the ability to write, we no longer had to sit around the campfire for hours listening to history. Historians recorded all the knowledge and legends of the time. We could consult the "library" of the time to get the information we needed.

Sagan points out that there must have been people who mourned the passing of the storytellers as a lost art, but at the same time, this new technology of recording history in writing freed us to be more inventive by giving us the time to think about how to improve the world we lived in. Instead of sitting around the fire for two hours listening, we suddenly had all this time on our hands. Humans, being curious and constantly poking a stick into something, used that spare time to create, discover, to invent new ways of doing things and new ways of thinking. The invention of the wheel may have come from that intellectual freedom.

And so it goes. Each innovation gives us more and more idle time. The human brain, being what it is, uses that time to be creative, inventive, and entrepreneurial.

In addition to the technological side of life, this spare time also frees us to search for answers to the unknown, to fill that vacuum in our minds. We developed theories about various gods controlling the forces of nature, human events like birth and death, and every other facet of our lives that had been cloaked in mystery at that time. That curiosity, that demand to have answers, is the reason why religion began and why it has been evolving. Before science and religion, our imagination was the only resource we had to unravel the mysteries of life.

Who?

Who did all this? Who is responsible for religion? The who question also begs the question of how things evolved in this discussion, so I will address them together. When we look at who did something, the companion question arises as to how they did what they did, why they did it, and eventually, where they did it.

And there you have the gist of what the 5 (or six) W's do for you when trying to untangle a mystery. The 'How' helps us understand the motivation of the who in a mystery. Sometimes, the where adds more information and when somebody did something. The W's can be examined independently, but they paint a more complete picture together.

We see this in TV detective shows that use the when, where, and how of a crime and the way it is committed – I am not calling religion a crime here - to discover who and sometimes why the crime was committed. Looking at how something is done (modus operandi) often gives the police a clue about the type of person who may have perpetrated the crime. The how helps define the suspect, or perp, as they like to say. Knowing how something came about and the circumstances that made it possible often assists in getting into the perpetrator's psyche.

That may seem confusing to some, but discussing the two issues together makes sense. As I warned early on, there will be overlap in other sections as well. I will endeavor not to make it too confusing.

Who? Who is God, or who were the gods of old? Who determined all of this to be? At this point, early in our evolution, let us call it a theory.

That brings up another side discussion. The word theory and theos are both gifts of the Greeks and the Greek language.

Theory is a contemplative and rational type of abstract or generalized thinking, or the results of such thinking as opposed to practice or fact.

Theos is the Greek word for a supreme being or God, yet there appears to be no known origin of the word Theos. I find that difficult to accept, given that the Greeks were so diligent about recording every damn thing they said or developed. One has to wonder if there isn't, or wasn't, a connection between the word that means generalized thinking with an absence of fact and the belief in an invisible god.

Back to the who question. For those times long past, we can only speculate how the story of religion played out since there are no written records. Still, the dynamics of a tribe, as most people existed back then and remain so today in many respects, would seem to paint a reasonable picture of how events might have unfolded.

After all, the human condition hasn't changed a great deal since the earliest of times. We are much more advanced technologically than our fur-bedecked ancestors. Still, as we hear the news of terrorists, cannibalism, infanticide, mass murder, and so on, it appears that we still live with a great many demons in our heads. When threatened or frightened, we tend to retreat to a place that promises peace and safety, our comfort zone, and we often rely on whatever faith we embrace.

In those early days, we were wanderers hunting for meat, roots, and anything edible that crawled across our path that our stomachs would tolerate.

A tribe must have relied on the strongest people, most likely men (thus, most of the god figures are those of men), to hunt for game and protect the tribe from marauding beasts and, probably, other tribes that were on the move and who were more than willing to abscond with anything edible, along with our breeding stock, human and animal.

Like the other animals, we instinctively understood the need to diversify the gene pool. Thus, the occasional camp raid focused on the ladies and children—another trait we share with the other animal groups.

The warrior and hunter positions in the tribe were positions of power, influence, and, I suspect, privilege. The tribe, after all, relied heavily on these men for their survival. These warrior types, like powerful and influential people today, most likely had their way with the tribal assets, both human and property; they could name their price, so to speak. They probably enjoyed their choice of mates, the lion's share of food, etc. It was a position of power and influence, and the trappings of all this power were most likely coveted by those not part of that powerful inner circle.

The fame associated with these prestigious positions must have created envy and competition for them. Other men who believed they were equal to or better than those in positions of power almost certainly challenged the leaders, as they do in most of the non-human world.

We still do this in the modern world in sports, business, and politics. Any profession that promises admiration, power, and money is the Petrie dish for this intrigue. We also see this same struggle for dominance between religions.

As we wandered about the known world at the time, encountering the forces of nature and the mysteries of life, birth, death, illness, and disease, the warrior class was helpless against the colossal events of nature. They were left without an explanation or an identifiable foe with whom to do battle.

They could only solve problems that required bravery, brute strength, and perhaps a sharp spear, all of which were ineffectual against the forces of nature and the universe, forces that left the masses paralyzed, quaking in fear, and looking for solace. They needed a leader and defender against such mysteries.

Due to their strength of numbers, these warriors could usually take on the fiercest beast and win. But they were helpless when it came to intellectual questions and challenges. They couldn't do battle with ideas and theories; at least the majority of them were incapable of engaging in a battle of wits, or they would still be the ruling class today.

At some point, a true intellectual of their time, not quite like today's intellectuals but brilliant nevertheless in the context of living in the Stone Age, pondered many of these questions and events that continued to plague and paralyze ancient civilizations.

I think whoever these thinking people were, must have announced to all who would listen that mysterious forces and entities existed, perhaps even calling them gods if such a word existed in their vocabulary, who were far more powerful than any warrior or even the tribal Chief. This had to be a message that the warriors and politicians found unsettling and threatening to both parties.

We know that many ancient civilizations believed in some invisible power. For some, it was an imagined spirit or many spirits, and for some, it was the wonders of nature, such as wolves or bears. The need for humans to assign responsibility for any act has been part of our being since the beginning of time.

The intellectual or seer who began talking about these gods might have been a shaman or chemist who had learned the secrets of plants and herbs to cure ailments, increase fertility, etc., making them revered tribe members.

Whoever this person or persons were, they must have stepped forward, perhaps in a clan meeting around the fire in the cave's relative safety, claiming to hold a "knowledge" of the unknown. It might have been the dreamer or the dream expert in the tribe.

Some civilizations, then and now, put great stock in dreams and in those who claimed to see what others could not or had the power to interpret our dreams.

They must have explained that these entities, these powerful gods no one could see, were responsible for all of life's otherwise unexplainable events.

Imagine everyone sitting around a fire in the cave after a meal of roots, berries, and perhaps a little meat from a careless animal that had wandered past. Everyone feels both satiated and curious about the world in which they live, and curiosity is one of the traits our emerging brain has developed.

Assume there had been a massive electrical storm that day that scared the daylights out of everyone and drove them inside the cave, where they felt safe but still quaked in fear.

Story-time - an anecdote

The fire crackles in the middle of the cave, casting eerily moving shadows of the tribe members on the cave walls. The smoke spirals to the cave roof and works its way across the ceiling to the notch carved above the door opening, allowing the smoke to escape without choking the tribal members.

Two old tribal members sit against a rock near the fire for warmth. Everyone in the tribe helps these wise old folks by bringing them food and water and attending to their every need; they are very close to death.

Children play inside the cave with sticks and rocks, engrossed in a game that only they understand and mainly oblivious to the adults' activities. Several women are repairing torn fur robes while carefully watching their children play.

The fire tender pokes at the fire to keep it strong. A hot ember rolls from the fire near the feet of one of the tribesmen. The fire tender, with practiced expertise, licks his fingers, picks up the ember, and, in a split second, returns it to the fire to the amusement and amazement of the tribe.

One of the elders, we shall call him Cormac – who knows how they referred to each other? — had been thinking about this problem of fear and ignorance by the tribal members for a long time.

Cormac perceived that to continue to evolve and move beyond their meager existence, people had to feel more comfortable leaving the cave to explore the world. He might have even been chewing on some particular plant that provided clarity not ordinarily present in other tribe members, rather like the Peruvians with their cocoa leaves. Cormac speaks to the tribe gathered around the fire. Some pay rapt attention, while others yawn. Cormac has a reputation for telling long stories.

> "We have seen how powerful the great sound and fire light
> in the sky can be."

He pauses to let that observation soak into the minds of these simple people. The women look up from their work while the children continue to play.

> "We have seen the fire light split a tree down the center. We
> have seen it strike one of us, swallowing our life to leave us
> smoldering like an ember in the fire. This kind of power and

destruction can only be the work of a mighty warrior — an angry warrior we have displeased in some way. We must find a way to atone for our transgressions."

The clan listens in silence, and then the tribal Chief, Yanda, feeling challenged by this sort of talk, speaks up.

"How does it happen that Cormac knows all this when no one else does?"

Cormac responds:

"It came to me in a vision a few suns ago. I have thought about it a great deal and believe it to be true. There can be no other explanation."

It was well known that Cormac was a man of visions who led his people to better hunting grounds and predicted events that no one else could imagine.

Of course, our language, or rather their language, like everything else back then, had yet to evolve very far, so my interpretation of the speech and use of words of the time enlists more than a bit of poetic license. Regardless, these pronouncements were likely met with a degree of skepticism and disbelief.

Some tribe members in our story turn to the Chief or the warriors, hoping to hear a counterargument. When none is offered, they begin to buy into the guru's story.

People shift uneasily in their spots around the fire, exchanging frightened looks, and burp and fiddle with everything around them, a typical display of agitation. It is hard to argue with the logic of such an important guru for the time. Yet, the ramifications of being at the mercy of this extraordinary power are frightening. The conversation continues as the Chief asks:

"What warrior, Cormac? Who is that strong?"

Dorbuk, the greatest warrior of the tribe, has a reputation for backing down from no man or beast, and he feels challenged by this explanation as he continues.

"Who is mightier than Dorbuk? Show me this warrior, and I will destroy him!"

Dorbuk is standing now, towering over the shorter Cormac and challenging him and all the other members of the tribe. Cormac replies:

"As I have said, therein lies the problem. No one can see the gods. They live far up in the sky from where they can throw down upon us the light that burns and kills. They hit the mighty log drum that shakes the ground to warn of their anger."

Dorbuk's eyes have narrowed to mere slits; his voice is now little more than a growl. He is confused as well as angry. No one could deny that the light and noise came from the sky.

"And how is it that you know this, Cormac?"

"As I said, I had a vision of them. The gods are taller than the tallest tree, and their voice is the great sound from the sky."

Knowing full well that Cormac is one of the tribe's gifted seers, he continues to press the issue.

"A vision? Why did only you have the vision?"

"It is my purpose to have visions and to share them with our people."

Cormac remains calm in the face of Dorbuk's storm. Dorbuk couldn't argue this point. While it was true that everyone had visions while they slept, only a few elders had the longevity and the gift to have visions used to guide the tribe. Still vexed, Dorbuk is determined to make Cormac look like a fool.

"Do these people, these so-called gods and mighty warriors, have names?"

True to his nature, Dorbuk does not give up without a fight. His fighting style is probing, looking for an opponent's weakness.

"Thor is The God of the big log-drum and burning light from the sky. All the gods have names."

True to his nature, Cormac had anticipated this question, but Dorbuk won't give in.

"How can you know their names?"

"I have spoken with some of the gods. They have come to me in a dream and told me their names. One day in the forest, when I was looking for roots, Thor spoke to me from a tree."

This declaration causes a murmur throughout the cave. Dorbuk is incensed. He can feel that he is losing his power over the people. Until now, Cormac only suggested the best places to gather food or pick out a cave for shelter. Now, he was challenging Dorbuk's position in the tribe by suggesting there was a higher and greater power than their head warrior, and the tribe was buying into this story. He knew he was helpless in the face of the forces of nature to either prevent them or explain why they happened.

The tribe members began talking among themselves about the gods, what they might look like, and how they might be appeased. Dorbuk stomps out of the cave.

By now, having overcome their initial shock, all the tribe members are leaning forward, hanging on every word that Cormac speaks and oblivious to Dorbuk. It is evident to all that Cormac possesses a level of knowledge that no one else has, and his power in the tribe is increasing as he speaks.

End of story

At last, as frightening as these gods were, there was an explanation for these terrible events that often plagued the tribe's people. Though mysterious, it was at least something to cling to. Cormac had indicated that Thor and the other gods are men who look like them, only much bigger.

If these gods were men, they must have a man's desires and appetites, and all they had to do was give them what they wanted to persuade them to stop the violence they rained down on their world. Not only that, but Cormac had some intimate knowledge of these gods, making him a powerful ally who might intervene on their behalf and a potential enemy for certain people in the tribe.

This is a condensed version of events that may have played out over several centuries, even millennia, for all we know. It is not a 10-minute discussion in a single cave. But for the purposes of this book, I've given you a 30-second historical drink from a fire hose.

Like most new ideas, Cormac may have been laughed at by some when he initially offered his explanation of the world. Some may have initially called him a madman.

He may have persisted until he was heard, or it may have taken generations of the Cormacs of the world pounding home this message before the masses began to believe the stories of gods.

Whether these philosophies came from a single source or multiple sources around the inhabited world of the time, motivated one suspects as a way to free people from fear, or whether the impetus was self-advancement and aggrandizement for the philosophers grabbing at the ring of power is unknowable. How they reached these conclusions, whether in a dream, a vision, or indulging in magic mushrooms, is also unknowable.

But like all new ideas, someone, or most likely multiple someones posited the notion of gods who controlled the unknown, and the idea caught on in the simple minds of these emerging and frightened human beings.

From this allegory, we can see the beginnings of the competition and sometimes conflict between the state or the government (in the form of the tribal Chief), the military (the warrior), and religion (the shaman or whoever began this discussion of higher powers).

Cormac's story of mighty gods controlling events and speaking only to specific individuals like himself endowed him with a unique power that no one else possessed, setting the stage for millennia of discord between religion and various branches of government.

Each competing human entity, the Chief, the warrior, and now the mysterious man of religion, is vying for the trust and, yes, the worship, love, or at least allegiance of the people. All three branches of power have existed in a tenuous partnership, and sometimes outright warfare, since the beginning of recorded history and the birth of religion.

It is difficult for an army to be religious and warriors simultaneously, carrying out the brutal acts often required of an army at war. When they have marched under the banner of the church, they have found themselves at odds with the teachings of most churches, forcing them to cherry-pick the passages from the texts that would justify the killing and carnage they felt they were obligated to heap on their victims in conquest.

Some passages of religious dogma were penned by these men who had participated in battles, knowing they needed to form a basis for cooperation with the other branches of government and the dominant religion of their time and region.

Any church that professes to believe in a loving, forgiving, and merciful God must also interpret its texts in a way that allows it to consent to the excesses and degenerate behavior of conquering armies and power-hungry politicians. Given the world when the Old Testament was authored, this might explain why the volume is so violent in dealing with life.

Most likely, the church did not lose sight of the fact that a conquering army could bring vast throngs of potential converts to their particular version of religion, whether slaves or conquered people. The more people they could get under their theological wing, the greater their influence, power, and potential wealth.

I know that last statement will make some religious zealots a little crazy. Still, anyone who thinks that religion is not a business, albeit presumably non-profit, is kidding themselves. Land and buildings are not free. All those vestments and gold-plated chalices are seldom donated to the church. And there are the clerics' salaries and others working behind the scenes in the offices. Yes, there may be a few volunteers, like the organist, but running a church costs money, and those at the top never lose sight of that. The stories of churches allied with politicians and wealthy people are legion.

History is replete with churches that felt threatened by another religion thrust on them by a conquering invader. Granting themselves absolution from all they had held sacrosanct, they conspired with the new government and the army to ensure their personal survival and, in so doing, were assured that they maintained control of their flocks.

If that meant making a preemptive strike on their foe, then so be it. They would find a way to turn it into their particular God's will. Wrapping the need for violence in one God or another went a long way to soothing the consciences of those involved and dismissing the misgivings of those who followed.

If you seek evidence of this, you only have to do some reading on Manifest Destiny as applied in the United States in the 19th century. This doctrine allowed the Europeans to settle in the United States of America in the early days and swarm over Mexico and Central and South America, committing genocide against the Native Americans in the western hemisphere. These conquerors either believed they were doing God's work or used it as an excuse to rape and pillage on a level seldom seen before or since, while compiling for themselves acres and acres of land and untold riches.

As that old saying so aptly states, "Politics makes strange bedfellows." We could probably amend that to say, "Politics and religion make strange bedfellows."

Make no bones about it: the machinations of churches and religion over the centuries have been about politics, wealth, and survival. This is not to imply that the followers of one religion or another weren't or aren't devout, but faced with extinction, they will find room in their dogma to accommodate whatever is required to ensure their survival and convince themselves that their God will approve of their actions.

To use a blatantly abused term from a sadly popular TV network, I prefer not to mention, in the interest of fair and balanced reporting, many within the Catholic Church of Spain opposed the mistreatment of the natives, Bartolome de Las Casas being one of the most prominent.

For the military and the politicians who have their empires to protect, serve, and expand, misinformation is the bulwark of these institutions. Having the church and its followers on your side made the task easier. They had the ear of large groups of people in their cathedrals and churches. The art of empire building has proven to be endemic in human nature, manifested in organizations large and small, be those governments, religious groups, or corporations.

The Role Of Men In Religion

And almost everything else. You may have noticed in my previous discussions that all the players have been men, a recurring theme in this exploration of religion and reaching for power. The truth is that the institutions of power, political, military, religious, and corporate, were developed by men and have been and still are primarily run by men for the ultimate benefit of men.

All the rules are lined up to make men's lives more comfortable and to downgrade and degrade all who would pretend to be their equals, with a historical focus on women. The groups that have been marginalized over history have included women, people of color, and other religions, or, more accurately, any other religion, nationalities, etc. Depending on what the dominant religion might be at any given time or place, all others are reduced in the eyes and minds of followers of that dominant religion.

Embedded in those dominant institutional cultures are the human traits that have defined our species from its beginnings, namely desire, power, greed, and the instinct to become increasingly powerful and influential. Ironically, religions have the audacity to preach against the sins of power and greed while being guilty of using these for their survival and grandeur.

Like the animals from whence we came, climbing to the pinnacles of our hierarchy is a driving force for humans. The who's who of religion is almost entirely dominated by men. Was it always so? Were women the first to conjure up the idea of gods, at least in some parts of the world? We can't know that for sure because there are no written records beyond a certain time into our past, and so far, no archeological artifacts to indicate definitively what might have happened.

You will find stories on the Internet, theories, and a degree of wishful thinking claiming that women ruled societies from Peru to Russia. That may be true, but from what I have read, no objective evidence of that yet exists.

If women were at the forefront of developing religion, it is my guess that men hijacked the idea. There are a few references to women in Christianity. For instance, there are seven prominent women in the New Testament: Mary, mother of Jesus; Mary Magdalene; Lydia of Phoebe; Mary of Bethany; Priscilla; and Junia. Contrast that with the twelve disciples and some forty other men mentioned in the New Testament. There are no female priests in Catholicism.

Buddhism prominently mentions a number of women, eight, I believe, but there has never been a female Dalai Lama. Women as monks have been very controversial. The good news is that the current Dali Lama thinks it is time for a female Dali Lama, but then some people wonder if he isn't the last of the Dali Lamas. Buddhism is evolving as well.

It is common knowledge that in much of Islam, women are denied even the most basic of human rights afforded non-Muslim women around the world, activities as simple as driving a car in Saudi Arabia. Conditions for women are improving and evolving, but very slowly and in isolated pockets of that religion, but not yet universally within Islam.

The Muslim men, on the other hand, appear to be, for the most part, free of most of the restrictions levied on the ladies. The rules are there, but since men wrote the rules, they seem to believe it is their right to break them.

In strict Muslim societies, women are never to go out alone, and young men and women can't "date." The wearing of burkas is well-known all over the world. One is obligated to wonder about the strict Muslim requirement of wearing a burka. On second thought, it's not a mystery at all. It is a man's world and has been for a long time.

Again, I come from a point of simple logic. I go back to the beginnings of Islam, some 600 years after the birth of Jesus. While having made advances, the world was still backward by today's standards. It must have been obvious then, as it is now, to those who were even the slightest bit observant that some men, perhaps many men, appeared incapable or unwilling to control their sexual urges.

I cannot help but wonder if this wasn't the perception that men wanted everyone to accept, the notion that these poor helpless men with testosterone coursing through their bodies, who faced down fearsome beasts and mighty warriors, were rendered helpless to exercise even a modicum of self-control in the company of attractive women.

This was an extension of men, creating a world that was favorable to and protective of men who might behave badly. That attitude gave rise to sayings like, boys will be boys. That is not parenting; that is enabling young boys to misbehave and have it sanctioned by the dominant adult males in society.

If a woman was showing any part of her skin, men might be aroused. The solution was to make women cover up — head to toe, no matter how hot and miserable they might be. It never seemed to occur to men that it might be their responsibility to reign in their urges, to begin to take responsibility for their behavior and actions. It was easier to blame loose women - women who were "asking for it" by dressing provocatively.

While no one, least of all men, wants to admit this is a systemic problem with men, the evidence is there when you look at countries like India, China, and the Middle East that are actively trying to teach boys and young men that they don't have the right to take a woman whenever they want. They have programs instructing men that women are equal, human, and deserve respect.

At this point, I want to interject a personal story to illuminate my point about male behavior and responsibility. I have been summoned for jury duty twice in my life. The first exercise went nowhere. I sat around for two days and was sent home.

The second invitation found me potentially on a jury in an accused rape trial. The accused was a black man, and the petitioner was a young white woman, a potentially volatile state of affairs, even in our semi-enlightened society around the year 2000.

We were going through voir deer, the process whereby attorneys, prosecuting and defense alike, ask prospective jurors questions to seat a jury they believe will be favorable for their client.

The defense attorney asked me something like whether a woman could dress provocatively enough that it suggested: "She wanted it." My response was that I found the question insulting to me as a man.

I went on to explain that if a drop-dead gorgeous woman walked through the courtroom stark naked right at that moment, while I might admire her or even be aroused and desire her, I had no right to act on those feelings. I said men must control their emotions and behavior, and any suggestion that we are helpless to do so was, in my opinion, an insult to male intelligence and our ability to control our emotions.

Having mounted my soapbox to make my speech to the defense attorney, who, I assumed, was looking for jurors who were sympathetic to his client being tempted by a loose woman, I figured I was toast as far as jury duty was concerned.

To be clear, I did not make my speech to dodge jury duty, but to express an opinion that I still hold today. To my surprise, I ended up on the jury.

The trial and deliberations went on for four or five days, and in the end, we had a hung jury—11 for acquittal and 1 for guilty. The rest of us were sure the one holdout had a hidden agenda, but our system, being what it is, required a unanimous 12-0 verdict. That was not the case, so a mis-trial was declared.

Thus, I believe we have the burka in Islam to make life easier for men at the expense of women. And it's not only the Muslims who cling to this notion that men are helpless and the victims of feminine beauty. In the early days of Christianity, with Luther and other religious leaders preaching from the pulpit, women were required to wear bonnets when they went out, as well as ankle-length dresses meant to obscure their vulgar and tempting figures and sensual body parts like their hair, neck, and ankles.

In many early American churches, men and women, even if married, were not allowed to sit together at Sunday services, just like Muslims today. The men and boys sat on one side and the women on the other. Today, some Christian sects like the Quakers and Mennonites require the women to sit in the back seat of the buggy or car if they drive one, while the men, obviously superior, sit in the front seat.

Could all this denial of human sexuality and oppression have anything to do with what seems to be almost an epidemic of rape, pedophilia, and bestiality, attributable in large part to men in society? Is this denial of natural human sexuality equivalent to forbidding young people access to alcohol until the age of 21? At this time, they go berserk and begin to binge-drink, some at an even earlier age.

Are we literally dangling candy in front of our children while denying them the pleasure of tasting the candy? Adults can drink and have sex and talk about how much they love to do both, all while denying that young men and women are capable of dealing with such things.

Nothing is more seductive than a Christmas present wrapped in such a way that you cannot divine the contents. It drives all of us a little crazy. We have had a debate for years about sex education in the United States. On the one side are those who believe it should be taught as a natural human emotion, along with teaching respect and responsibility. On the other side are the burka crowd.

Again, we are talking about rules made by men to make life easier for men. To continue, Judaism, Sikhism, and the list of religions discriminating against women is long. But why is this so universally true? This is a question better put to a psychologist or a sociologist, but I will not let that get in my way of offering a possible answer.

The subjugation of women is as old as history itself. If we rewind to our earliest beginnings when very little separated us from our animal cousins, the males most likely dominated the females when we came together to mate, as still happens in much of the animal kingdom.

Being, for the most part, bigger and stronger, and given the male role in society requiring that they range over vast areas of land hunting wild animals and fighting other tribes, the males likely lorded it over the females until it was time for them to leave and wander their world, hunting and sleeping, returning for the next mating season to fight off other males and mate as often as they could.

The dominance of men has been debated for centuries. We can look at our ancient history, as well as our genetic links to other primates in general, for part of the answer.

Other than stumbling upon injured or recently deceased game as we wandered the land in tribes, the way we might stumble on road kill today, and before we settled into more permanent camps and embraced an agrarian culture, those mighty hunters had to go searching for game so that their clan might eat and survive. This arduous task of walking miles over rough terrain, bringing down sometimes large animals, dressing them in the field, and then hauling all that back to camp required a good deal of strength and developed strength in those who lacked it.

Was there ever a time when men and women were physically equal? When women had the same muscle mass as men? Not that I'm aware of, but there may have been pockets of civilization around the world where this was the case, and archaeologists still need to uncover the evidence. It does appear, and we can draw a general conclusion that, like most of the animal kingdom, the males are bigger and stronger than the females.

This is likely nothing more than the product of natural selection. Perhaps in the very early days, some men and women were equal in almost every way, and those societies that failed to survive did so because one of the sexes wasn't more powerful and superior. Men might have been more like women in terms of physical stature. Other species, where the males evolved to be larger and took on roles that required greater strength, like hunting and defense, had more success. We may be the result of that evolution and survival of the fittest.

Whether we've been that way forever, or whether evolution determined our roles in response to the demands and dangers in a world where other, often larger and stronger animals were also searching for food, it would have been insane for a single male armed only with a stone-tipped tree branch, to go out alone searching for game, so we used hunting parties, a group perhaps of four, five, or six of our mightiest warriors to hunt, kill, and drag home some large carcass for the tribe to eat.

One can imagine that moving only on foot and even employing the fastest of the men, these forays required being away from the tribe for many days at a time, depending on the success of the hunt. This had to have had the effect of creating people, men and women both, who were not only comfortable with a degree of solitude but a situation that engendered a strong sense of individuality and separateness. At the same time, it required teamwork to succeed, whether you stayed back at the cave or ventured out to hunt game in teams.

Many of these traits are apparent today, notably in modern American males and perhaps males in general. We have only to look at sports teams with wildly out-of-control egos at times, a willingness to push your body to the limits coupled with physical superiority, strong personalities, a passion for competition, and the knowledge that working as a team is the only way to succeed to see how our ancestors might have genetically molded us.

While it was true that the men would go out on hunting parties, it was also true that there was a high probability that one or more of them might not return. Falling prey to dangers such as wild beasts, poisonous snakes, or accidental tumbles over a cliff was inevitable and generally fatal.

It seems to me that the men, while developing a camaraderie and a sense of teamwork necessary to the success of any hunting mission, might have also avoided forming too close a bond with the others that could turn out to be psychologically crippling should that person meet an untimely end.

Going back to my sports analogy, you hear about players who "are on the bubble." These are players trying to make the team, but who may have fewer physical talents or are unlucky enough to be stuck behind a superstar who plays the same position.

These players on the bubble, who may be immensely popular with the other players, must sense that the other players who "have it made" are avoiding making too close a bond with those who may be gone the next day. The last thing the tribe or a sports team needs is a whimpering and mourning warrior huddled in the cave, too depressed to function when the hunt or the game is on the line, or a person who lets the team down in the face of danger out on the plain.

If, in fact, men existed like this for tens of thousands of years or even longer, it had to have affected the male psyche, effectively rewiring our brains so that we were better suited to survival in the wild and able to cope with our role as solitary hunters or warriors than the communal traits needed in society.

This is not meant to excuse modern men for bad behavior, but rather to explain the evolution — there's that word again — that likely led to the males in society dominating both the content and execution of religious dogma and seldom seeking the counsel of others.

To a large degree, men were and remain solitary individuals with limited bonding skills who have a natural flair for leadership, or at least the desire to be in charge. Not every man is like this, but the traditional male role over the centuries has developed or evolved in a way that has wired our brains based on our roles that traditionally have required aggressiveness and a take-charge attitude.

Like any other animal society, we can't all be in charge, so we have the inevitable battles of will, wit, and sometimes physical encounters to sort out the hierarchy within society at all levels, be it political, corporate, or on the sports field. We call it competition, and it exists in every layer of society, including religion.

To be sure, we have moved a long way beyond those hunting parties. Common sense would dictate that we should have abandoned many of those traits centuries ago. Still, ten, twenty, or thirty thousand years or more of conditioning will not be undone in a handful of generations.

Most men don't flourish in an environment of consensus or teamwork but one of strong individuality and competitiveness. They will follow team rules if they see a personal benefit but are still rugged individuals. These are the ones who percolate to the top in both business and politics and some of whom, long ago, recognized they could reach an exalted position in society by becoming involved in and in charge of religion. The men who are warm and fuzzy and committed to consensus become consultants. That should garner me some angry emails.

With the changes in corporate culture in the last few decades and an emphasis on self- and participative management, some of the old-school managers from those rugged, individualistic bygone days have struggled with the concept of consensus and even teamwork, let alone women in authority. Slowly but surely, they are falling by the wayside, like the old warrior who is too arthritic to go out on a hunt or into battle.

There is evidence that some of the younger generation of males get it and are evolving toward a society with greater emotion and the skills to coexist and negotiate rather than to start cussing and hurling abuses, ready to throw down and fight for superiority at the slightest provocation.

When they returned from dangerous missions, our ancestors, those mighty warriors of yesteryear, brought armloads of meat back to the den. They lived a life of luxury, taking what they wanted in return for their efforts.

Think of modern events like the Super Bowl, where our victorious warriors return from battle with the ultimate prize, the Lombardi Trophy. They are literally treated like Greek Gods. They are lauded by the fans, given parades, paid vast sums of money to do commercials for consumer products, and end up having their contracts renegotiated for even more money.

All of this male activity, then as now, left the women at home with the children, often pregnant, to shift for themselves as best they could until the men returned. This means, first and foremost, one assumes that the responsibility for the children in the tribe belonged to the women since they obviously were not allowed to go on a hunt with the men, especially dragging small children with them.

As you often see today, women came together to form a network of support, something rarely seen in males. True, males will stand shoulder to shoulder and fight off a threat from either man or beast, but they typically do not bond the way women do.

The women had to look after other women nearing childbirth when they were most vulnerable, an undertaking perhaps as difficult and frightening as facing a fearsome beast. In their spare time, they had to forage for food to feed the tribe, do a little hunting of their own if the men were long away, and perhaps even ward off intruders from other tribes as well as predatory animals. They were by no means weak or helpless.

The fact that they were often smaller in stature and, in most cases, not as physically powerful engendered a sense of teamwork based on the knowledge that, alone, they were vulnerable, but together, their numbers could overcome many challenges and ensure the survival and success of their tribe.

Millions of years of this kind of responsibility and conditioning engineered ancient female brains to seek companionship, work together, and nurture each other. They also taught their children the rudiments of survival and how to live together in a group or tribe, a lesson that modern men are still struggling to embrace.

Women often function better in corporations and politics, where cooperation and negotiation trump confrontation. At the same time, women can struggle with the individualism and perhaps aggression that have defined the typical male role, be that in the corporate, sports, or political world. That, too, is changing.

Like the men, they are fighting a millennium of conditioning that has hard-wired their brains to survive in their given roles. However, they now must try to adopt new behaviors to function in a new world. And they are succeeding in that endeavor, as seen in politics, the corporate world and the emergence of women in sports.

The purpose of these last few paragraphs is not intended to piss anyone off, though it might. It demonstrates that the males, who were dominant in most of the clans' business, were not going to easily surrender their position of authority to this new idea of these gods, these mysterious beings who were all-powerful and invisible if you were to accept the premise that such powerful and omnipotent creatures existed.

As this new philosophy took root in people's minds, the men who proffered this new way of looking at the world knew they had to own this idea to remain in power or to seize it from those who currently were in charge.

Indeed, the proponents of religion must have championed the theory with enthusiasm and passion. At the same time, those in established positions of power, such as the military or government, felt threatened and resisted the idea.

The intellectuals pushing this theory of gods were the equivalent of today's nerds or geeks, at least according to these men, who relied on bluster and force to win the day. This battle started a long time ago and continues today.

Whether these dominant-type males hijacked religion from the meeker members of society or from the more intellectual members of the tribe, the men or women who may have first posited the ideas, or whether they were, in fact, the original architects of a belief in supernatural beings controlling everyone's lives would seem almost impossible to verify.

What is true is that almost every religion has been, and still is, dominated by men. God is presumed to be a man. Jesus was a man. Mohammed, Buddha, and the majority of major players in all the religions on the planet were men. Men wrote the Bible, Torah, and Quran. It would seem that God chose to speak only to men.

In the story of Adam and Eve, it is written that God created Adam first — in His own image. As something of an afterthought, He decided to "give" Adam a woman. Pay close attention to the language used to describe many of these events found in the Bible. Read how God came to create women and tell me a man did not write that part.

To spare you looking this part up in your Bible, I'll give you a synopsis of what it says.

> "But no suitable helper was found for Adam. So, the Lord God caused the man to fall into a deep sleep. While he was sleeping, he took one of the man's ribs and closed up the place with flesh. Then the Lord God made a woman from

the rib he had taken out of the man, and he brought her to
the man."

Then along came the serpent to tempt not Adam but Eve. The serpent
succeeded, and God raised all sorts of hell. After ripping the snake a
new one, he continued:

To the woman, he said,

> "I will make your pains in childbearing very severe; with
> painful labor, you will give birth to children. Your desire will
> be for your husband, and he will rule over you."

The woman is defined as "his helper." It was Eve, not Adam, who was
tempted into sin. And "he will rule over you". Can you imagine that
story written by anyone but a man? If a woman had written the myth
about creation, how might it be read?

In any case, it would appear that religion was the device of men,
designed for men, documented by men, and remains primarily the
dominion of men to this day. All other human and non-human beings
are seen as something less than the almighty male.

Our Emerging Intellect

Let us return to our ancient relatives of yesteryear, who were evolving beyond their reptilian brains, which were dominated to a large extent by such stimuli as hunger, heat, and cold, in response to a world where fight or flight dictated many of their actions.

We were slowly moving to a higher form of intellect with a brain that began questioning our world. The evolution of a form of religion with religious thought or a form of spiritualism is a logical step in that progress.

As a species, we were developing strong familial bonds — other animals do this as well, and lifelong bonds and emotions like love, hate, jealousy, and greed, which seem less prevalent in the rest of the animal kingdom.

Many of these feelings may have already existed, but our reptilian brains had no way to process what we were feeling. Among these emotions was a sense of loss when a loved one died. Our newly formed, or forming brain now demanded not only answers to death but answers that alleviated the pain of our loss.

This is not to imply that ancient people over 50,000 years ago didn't feel a sense of loss when someone in the tribe died. Still, their brains must have dealt with such events more on the level of a chimpanzee or even lesser intellects than modern humans. Death had no context. We were curious why a person had stopped moving. We most likely poked at them, smelled them, made sounds to try to arouse them, and felt a sense of loss, but we quickly moved on just as most animals do in the wild.

Love and death are not uniquely human emotions. There is ample evidence in other primates, as well as many animal species that bond for life and who appear to mourn the loss of their mates and family - that they share many of our senses of attachment and loss. Emotions are not exclusive to the human species.

Swans, beavers, wolves, and even termites mate for life. I won't go down that path here. Still, I encourage the listener to discover more about animal emotions if they are interested in the topic.

Many animals appear to mourn the death of one of their own. Elephants mourn death, but dolphins, geese, chimpanzees (no surprise since we share about 99% of our genetic makeup with them), and even scrub jays hold a kind of funeral.

But humans alone have turned death into an industry, a lucrative one to be sure, with funeral homes, caskets, cemeteries, crematoriums, and various complex ceremonies. And, true to form, when death became the domain of the gods and then the one God, the church played a significant role in how death was perceived, mourned, and tried to define what followed death.

Another quick interjection. We humans want ceremonies in our lives. Whether it is the pomp and ceremony of royal families, religion, Thanksgiving Day parades, or watching the Oscars presentation ad nauseam on television, we get some reassurance that all will be well from these ceremonies.

The ancient ones existed in a hostile world full of events that were far beyond their comprehension: earthquakes, hurricanes, tornados, drought, blizzards, all the forces of nature that could, and often did, prove deadly to their clan. Add to that wild animals, and yes, even other humans who had no compunction about bopping a fellow human on the head to abscond with their food, furs, or their women, and it is no big stretch to imagine that a degree of chaos must have been part of everyday life back then.

The thinkers of the time must have seen or sensed a need to create a sense of order in society that had not been achieved through the rule of law alone, the threat of physical punishment, or simple common sense. Something more compelling was called for to get all these people in line, and that something was religion.

This desire to have everyone embrace a philosophy of behavior must have been one of the ingredients, and perhaps a main ingredient, in the cauldron of ideas that would develop into what became the recipe for what we know as religion today.

That is another human instinct or trait. We want everyone to march in a straight line. We get very nervous when it appears that no one is in control. We don't like people who run out of bounds or color outside the lines. We want a plan, someone calling the shots, everyone playing by the rules, and then we are happy, at least until they screw up, then we want them out of our lives. Occasionally, each of us wanders off the game board, but we usually find a way to justify our behavior

I saw an example of that when I became a manager at Boeing. We were going through what most companies had dubbed a cultural change. American industry was moving from the model based on autocratic rule of the 19th and a good part of the 20th centuries, where threats and intimidation were considered motivators (fire one person each month whether they deserved it or not to keep the attention of all the others), to a participative, more democratic approach to running a business. The idea was that the people doing the work, some of whom would one day be managers, could participate in decisions that had previously been in the management domain.

I was heavily involved and committed to the revolution, and upon becoming manager, I met with my group and offered an organization chart that broke from the typical hierarchical pyramid chart, presenting one that looked more like the Knights of the Round Table. I was trying very hard to be participative and get away from the idea that I was above them.

Within each box was a person's name and job title, so it was obvious I was the manager—the label said so—but my name didn't set god-like at the top of some pyramid. I asked the group to consider this approach, and we would get together in a couple of days to decide.

The result was that people preferred something other than my new approach. In our discussions, there was talk of wanting to know who the decision maker was. They wanted a hierarchy, possibly so they didn't have to worry about making and being responsible for decisions, and so the blame for failure could be accurately applied to the person at the top. Or maybe this was too much, too fast, and moving them out of their comfort zone. To my knowledge, no one else in the company was doing this: I was asking them to color outside the lines. There is comfort in group thinking. We kept the old model of the organization chart.

To this day, I don't know if it was simply too much, too fast, or just a sucky idea that I had failed to sell to the group.

If the rules of life and morality were set by a deity or deities who were declared to be without flaws, then unlike the leaders behind man-made laws who were breaking their own rules right and left, there was at least a chance that followers would abide by the rules set by these all-powerful, and occasionally vengeful gods, thus saving society from itself.

As discussed earlier, there had to have been free thinkers all along. These people sought answers for the events that visited humans and evolved the notion that such powerful forces of nature had to be the work of powerful entities, unseen forces at work. They couldn't just happen by magic or circumstance; someone or something had to be behind these events and bring them to pass for a reason.

This desire to know, or at least have a plausible explanation for the unknown, continues today as we seek to overcome disease, venture further into the cosmos, and pursue science and technology on every front to push back the frontiers of ignorance. The human thirst for knowledge and understanding is one of the most potent forces that has driven our species forward faster and further than any other animal we know.

Our concept of the world and universe is much different from the one in which our ancestors lived and died. At the time, their knowledge was limited to those events they could witness without the aid of science or theories. The unexplained, like weather anomalies, scared the hell out of people.

Powerful men like the warriors and hunters in our clan represented our best defense against the physical threats presented by animals and other humans. It was natural that we would imagine that the deities who were behind the giant forces of nature should take the form of humans. Our imaginative pallet was limited to only what we could see and experience in the small world in which we traveled — our sphere of knowledge was limited to our physical world, which was limited to the area we could cover on foot.

Gods had to take human form because we were incapable of visualizing anything else. The possibility of other planets existing, let alone ones like the one we inhabited, was simply not on our radar screen.

The idea of planets populated by little green men with bulging eyes was millennia away. The minds of our ancient ancestors couldn't begin to conjure up such images. That would have to wait thousands of years for the discovery of other planets and the science fiction writers who would eventually stimulate our imaginations and bring other planets and aliens to life, albeit mostly imagined.

The gods' voices were thunder; their anger, earthquakes and lightning, blizzards, forest fires, and hurricanes were all signs of their irritability. Their benevolence was the rain and sun that insured our food supply and their ability to make us fertile to bear children or take them away if they so chose.

Imagine the fear that must have ruled our existence. These gods were seen as men, and with few exceptions, were almost always men who used their incredible powers to punish humans for unimaginable transgressions.

These transgressions were identified by the burgeoning leaders of religion, conjured up as part of their dogma based on their personal moral standards. It contributed to their grab for power, using fear of the unknown and retribution to gain influence over their followers and bring them into line with their personal set of values.

To appease these gods, we developed rituals to honor and worship them, hoping to diminish their anger. These rituals led to the sacrifice of animals and even to the sacrifice of humans in some cultures. This could explain, in part, some of the legends surrounding the death of Jesus on the cross. There can be little doubt that he was crucified, but the rest of his mystery is open for question.

Not that the Romans embraced human sacrifice, they didn't. In fact, they abhorred the practice, but death nailed on a cross was okay. They considered themselves religious, and their beliefs were dominated by the multiple god theory.

So, in addition to the story, real or imagined, that Jesus proclaimed himself king - he purportedly alluded to being the son of God - it was an act of heresy, according to the Jews.

This made him a double threat, according to the government of Rome. Their allegiance with the Jews was tenuous at best, and this upstart Jew was screwing things up by the numbers. If he were to convince the Jews that he really was the long-awaited messiah, they would almost certainly turn away from the rule of Rome.

With his followers declaring him the son of God, a claim, by the way, that was written down centuries after Jesus was dead, I am left wondering how much of what is attributed to him was ever said by him.

I remain skeptical that Jesus made such a claim. He is purported to have referred to his Father in heaven, a comment that, if true, I believe was a euphemism. Christians pray, "My Father, who art in heaven . . . " Does anyone reciting that prayer consider themselves the literal son or daughter of God?

God was and is the heavenly Father of all who believe in Him. Jesus's crucifixion and then his declaration that he rose from the dead and ascended into heaven to be with his Father prompted his followers to see these developments as the ultimate sacrifice by God and believe that his death absolved people of their sins.

Before anyone starts looking for a Mikey-sized bucket full of hot tar, let me hasten to say that Jesus was a real person, and he did die on the cross. I'm convinced of that, but as for the rest of the story, as my friend Father Schwab said, "You either believe or you don't."

In my world, that story has been distorted and embellished over the almost 2,000 years of storytelling. It seems likely to me that Jesus' loved ones and followers spirited his dead body away to give him a decent burial before the Romans dragged his carcass through the streets behind a chariot.

When, the following day, other folks came by the tomb and found the rock covering the tomb rolled aside, the myth of his rising from the dead and ascending into heaven was born, or perhaps invented by the culprits who absconded with his body to distract the Romans from looking for a grave thief. And, since those who took him away loved and revered him as their teacher, they were not inclined to dispel the mystery that was created and almost certainly took their secret to the grave. And like so many fantastic stories, the believers embraced the legend as fact.

It is unlikely that anyone will find his grave, and since, as far as we know, he had no relatives, there is no DNA to test. If we did find his grave, or if it has already been found, there is no shortage of people, including the Vatican in Rome, who would go to great lengths to keep that fact a secret.

Jesus was a rebel for his time. He agitated against not only the corruption within the Jewish temples and religion but also the oppressive rule of Rome. He also taught a philosophy that was decidedly different from the fire, and brimstone was presented in what we now call the Old Testament. He was a thorn in their side, pun intended. Anyone embarking on a path that involves challenging both the government and a major religion is not going to have a pleasant time of it, then or now.

That's why I'm limiting this work to a discussion of religion, except where I jump in with a story or a tangential opinion, which may be often. I expect that I will piss off enough people without enraging the conservatives in our nation, who will, I suspect, never hear this journey into the past and the vagaries of the human mind. They tend not to want to entertain new ideas and are fond of banning books that challenge their assumptions.

Jesus was and remains today one of the most important movers in humankind's history on this earth. Few people in history, if any, have had the impact on the world that this man named Jesus has had.

Offhand, only the Prophet Mohammed and Siddhārtha Gautama, The Buddha, seem to have affected so many people.

Instead of fire and damnation, as is often preached in the Old Testament, Jesus preached love and peace. He rejected the violence and called for killing those who offended you. He railed against the unholy alliance between the rabbis and the Roman government. He emphasized the moral obligation of those better off to help their neighbors who may be suffering. He disputed much of what was in the Old Testament and the accepted class distinctions of the time.

This made him both a heretic of those of the Jewish faith and a revolutionary according to Rome. It should surprise no one that they would want to silence him. For both the Jewish leaders and the Roman rulers, this man who rode on an ass was a pain in the ass and had to go.

It never fails to amaze me that good friends who are devout Christians will quote the New Testament but dismiss or simply ignore the Old Testament with its threats of retribution, support of slavery, and subjugation of women. Yet, they accept that Jesus was the son of God.

How can, or how do they reconcile that this revered son of God came to earth and began to debunk everything his Father is supposed to have said in the Old Testament? How do you reconcile that there is a God, the God of Abraham from the Old Testament, who is more powerful than Jesus? Yet, the two had dramatically different philosophies about life.

The website Religious Tolerance.org reports that there were at least two dozen competing belief systems that existed among Jews in the first century, the first third of a century that saw Jesus walking the earth. There were "Sadducees, Pharisees, Essenes, Zealots, followers of John the Baptist, followers of Yeshua of Nazareth (Iesous in Greek, Iesus in Latin, Jesus in English), and others. Each group was interpreting the

Hebrew scriptures and applying them to the world in which they lived. Again, this is an example of religion evolving and competing for the minds of people.

Why might the followers of the various Jewish sects who move toward Jesus have been receptive to a different point of view? Let's examine some of the proclamations from the Old Testament, the accepted word of God in most God-based religions, the one and only God and the Father of Jesus, as we look for a clue to the why and how of religion.

> The Lord thy God am a jealous God, visiting the iniquity of the fathers upon the children unto the third and fourth generation. Exodus 20:5

> For the LORD thy God is a consuming fire, even a jealous God. Deuteronomy 4:24

> I, the LORD thy God, am a jealous God, visiting the iniquity of the fathers upon the children unto the third and fourth generation. Deuteronomy 5:9 (There appears to be some repetition or plagiarism by the authors of these chapters)

> (For the LORD thy God is a jealous God among you) lest the anger of the LORD thy God be kindled against thee, and destroy thee from off the face of the earth. Deuteronomy 6:15

> They provoked him to jealousy with strange gods, and with abominations provoked him to anger. Deuteronomy 32:16

Wow! Whoever wrote Deuteronomy had some severe anger management issues.

He is a jealous God; he will not forgive your transgressions nor your sins. Joshua 24:19

I have to observe that this passage closely resembles what we call political talking points today. In modern times, and assuming you don't subscribe to the hardcore Islamic point of view, imagine living your life under the threat of various punishments, or even death, for behavior that we consider pretty standard today.

But the people calling the shots back then would find much of our behavior offensive, if not an abomination. Things like a man and woman walking together on the street, and worse yet, holding hands. I'm going to go out on a limb and suggest you might entertain changing your religious allegiances under these circumstances if a better option came along, and it appears that was the case with the Jews who followed Jesus.

The God of the Old Testament does not strike me as someone you might want to stop after work to grab a couple of beers or invite to your house for a Saturday barbecue. He is portrayed as jealous, angry, and vengeful, not unlike—no, I won't go there. I was going to get political in 2024 as I work on this.

Life for countless people back then was already hell on earth, with little hope of escaping from the life they found themselves in. It was the definition of a hardscrabble life if you were free and an abomination if you were a slave. To be threatened by this pissed-off God, along with all the other travails of surviving in an ancient world run mainly by tyrants of one sort or another, was too much for many folks to deal with on their own.

Enter the likes of John the Baptist and Jesus of Nazareth, who argued that there was a better way, a gentler way to believe in God, a benevolent God who was not bent on revenge but one who preaches forgiveness and inclusion.

Hey, life was a bitch as it was without having to worry about this angry God visiting some crap on you. To my knowledge, they never tried to explain how this God had suddenly switched from an angry and vengeful God to one full of love and forgiveness. It didn't matter because it was what people wanted to hear.

Between Christianity, Islam, and Judaism, Jesus is the subject of a good deal of debate. Did he exist? There can be no doubt. All three of these religions acknowledge his existence. He was real.

Remember for this discussion that all three religions believe in the same God, no matter what they might call Him. They all accept the stories of people like Abraham and Moses but differ greatly about who Jesus was. Was he the son of God? Two out of three of these religions say no. This sounds a little like a majority opinion to me.

The Christians declare that he was the son of God, the Messiah, as predicted by Judaism, the religion from which the Muslims, Christians, and Jesus himself emerged. Next, we should look at some of what the Bible claims Jesus said. Before getting into that, I should inject another thought, theory, or opinion—take your pick.

The New Testament was written some 300 years after Jesus was crucified. That represents many generations of storytelling. If you look at our modern civilization, where the average marrying age is 25 (I'm using 25 for this argument, although that varies widely around the world and is nothing more than my opinion on the average age for producing children), that 300-year span of time between when events supposedly occurred and when the story was finally written down as gospel represents twelve generations of storytelling, and wine was already a popular beverage.

That would be the same as if your great-great-great-great-great-great-great-great-great-great-great-great-grandfather had told a story in the 1700s that is passed down from person to person, often after a couple of drinks, until it reached you.

All of your ancestors, some sober and perhaps some not-so-sober, sitting around the kitchen table, repeating and embellishing the family history from one generation to another. How many revisions to the original story might have occurred? How many people with a vested interest in the tale, portraying Uncle Frank in a particular light, may have fudged the facts? How factual is the story that was eventually told to you? It may be a great story, but it may be fifty-percent bullshit.

Most of us must have played the game in school where the teacher whispered something in the ear of the first student in the first row of desks. Then, each student whispered to the one behind them what they thought they heard, and they, in turn, to the next student behind them, and so on. The last student in line then reported what they were told. The results from only ten minutes of storytelling between twenty-five students were both surprising and often hilarious.

So, the probability that what was written about Jesus 300 years after his death is factually accurate may hold the same probability as that of me being the reincarnation of James Joyce. We are both Irish, but beyond that, well . . .

I might also add that the Bible was written by a bunch of old men who also thought the world was flat, who most likely believed in witches and all sorts of spirits, and who thought that the stars revolved around our stationary world which, naturally, God placed at the center of the universe. God knows what other myths they might have embraced back then and how much these fears and demons altered their perception of what had been passed down to them.

So, back to what Jesus is reported to have said:

Jesus Said He Existed Before Abraham

> "Your Father Abraham rejoiced as he looked forward to my coming. He saw it and was glad."

The people said, "You aren't even fifty years old. How can you say you have seen Abraham?"

> Jesus answered, "I tell you the truth, before Abraham was even born, I Am!"

It seems evident to me that Jesus was saying that Abraham predicted his birth because of the myth that there would be a Jewish messiah. If Jesus, in fact, uttered these exact words, I doubt that he was saying he was as old as Abraham.

Jesus Said to See Him is the Same as Seeing God

> Jesus shouted to the crowds, "If you trust me, you are trusting not only me but also God who sent me. For when you see me, you are seeing the one who sent me. I have come as a light to shine in this dark world so that all who put their trust in me will no longer remain in the dark."

Jesus was asking for the people's trust. He believed man was created in God's image and was trying to enlighten them. He had to move these people from the dogma of the Old Testament to a new way of thinking. I suspect he may have had a bit of Elmer Gantry about him—you young folks might have to look Elmer Gantry up.

It's time for another of my interruptions with a real-life story. I once heard a report about a young athlete who is generally perceived as an astonishing quarterback. This athlete took our Seattle Seahawks to the

Super Bowl two years back-to-back, winning the first and narrowly missing the second.

If you still need to figure out who I am talking about, it is Russell Wilson. He was negotiating his contract in the bright light of his success of the previous three years, and understandably so. You know that every one of us would do the same thing.

In an interview, he said he wanted to stay in Seattle but that he had moved from one place to another in the past, presumably according to God's plan, and he would go wherever God wanted him to be. That is not an exact quote, but it is close.

I don't think anyone truly believes that God was talking personally to Russell or that God is plotting the details of Russell's football future. Sincerely religious people say things like that; it doesn't mean they have God's cell number or that He is texting them instructions on how to manage their lives and careers any more than the quotes that are attributed to Jesus, if they are accurate, should be taken literally and meant that God was talking to him.

> "No one can come to the Father except through me. If you
> had really known me, you would know who my Father is.
> From now on, you do know him and have seen him!"

You can hear similar preachings in modern-day churches. You have to come to church regularly and pray through whoever your church leader is because he or she has a more direct line, or so worshipers hope, and more influence on God in their lives, a kind of ecclesiastical hotline to heaven. The Pope, the leader of the Catholic Church, is believed by many to be closer to God than any human on earth. He is practically considered divine. And so it goes.

Jesus Said He Could Forgive Sins:

> "...that you may know that the Son of Man has authority on earth to forgive sins"—he then said to the paralytic—"Rise, pick up your bed and go home." And he rose and went home. When the crowds saw it, they were afraid and glorified God..."

I have a couple of problems with that particular passage. First, I would point out that it says, "the Son of Man." Is Jesus acknowledging that he is mortal? And healing the crippled, raising the dead, giving sight to the blind, all these stories seriously stretch probability.

These particular stories lob a brick into my intellect and stretch my imagination beyond reasonableness. I hope that most free-thinking people feel some of that. Either that or all the fire and brimstone faith healers hauling their tents and snakes around the country is the real deal.

> He said to them, "You are from below; I am from above. You are of this world; I am not of this world. I told you that you would die in your sins, for unless you believe that I am he, you will die in your sins."

This is another attempt, in my opinion, to convince the masses who were uneducated by today's standards that they have to follow the path that Jesus was laying out — he was, after all, a preacher, a teacher, a storyteller, and a philosopher. Telling them it was a better idea wasn't working all that well, considering the many opponents of Jesus were threatened by his sermons and his very different version of God's word than what had been accepted as fact for many centuries. Maybe Jesus tossed in some hyperbole to get their attention.

I don't know how much, if any, of Jesus' opposition's rebuttals were recorded for history. The zealots following Jesus were not likely to jot down statements against him if they jotted down anything. Still, you can be sure the propaganda was hot and heavy in both directions, pro and con, for Jesus. This isn't any different from our political parties arguing their varying points of view and stretching reality to make a point and bring people over to their side.

In the context of today's world, most of Jesus' pronouncements are very bold statements indeed, assuming this is, in fact, what Jesus said and not the work of revisionist memories by the religious zealots years later wanting to believe.

Let's look at some things that have been said by other modern religious leaders.

> "I think He showed me about the next president, but I'm not supposed to talk about that, so I'll leave you in the dark — probably just as well — but I think I know who it's gonna be," Robertson said on the Christian Broadcasting Network's "700 Club."

Most of us understand that Robertson was a little around the bend. In his later years, he was demented. Still, a good number of people took him at his word.

L. Ron Hubbard founded the Church of Scientology. He declared himself to be "Metteya" (Maitreya), the forthcoming world spiritual teacher and leader from the Buddhist poem Hymn of Asia.

George Baker, also known as Father Divine (you have to love that name), was an African American spiritual leader from about 1907 until his death in 1965. His full self-given name was Reverend Major Jealous Divine, and he was also known as "the Messenger" and George Baker early in his life. He founded the International Peace Mission movement, and Father Divine claimed to be God.

David Koresh, the leader of a Branch Davidian religious sect, proclaimed himself to be the final prophet.

Believe me, there is a long list of folks throughout history who have made such claims, and some of them are, well, humorous, to say the least, while others were evil and frightening.

This in no way is to suggest that Jesus was a charlatan — how can anyone know anything except what was written down 300 years after his death? Jesus did exist, and somewhere in all those writings is a kernel of truth about him and what he believed. If the Bible is to be believed, He preached peace, love, and tolerance, a message needed today as much, if not more, than any time in the past. It is also a lesson many of his self-proclaimed adherents today seem to have misplaced. And one would wish that radical sects of all religions would give more importance to what Jesus had to say.

How much of what those old men wrote down almost 2,000 years ago is accurate? No one can say with any certainty. Many of the quotes have multiple meanings, a parable, as they are often called. For reference, a quick definition of a parable

A parable is a succinct, didactic (enlightening/instructive/moral) story in prose or verse that illustrates one or more lessons or principles. It differs from a fable in that fables employ animals, plants, inanimate objects, or forces of nature as characters, whereas parables have human characters.

And finally, if someone were to go around today making similar statements about themselves or a religious leader they followed, we would quickly put them away on a steady diet of Prozac. They would be summarily dismissed as nut cases, as Pat Robertson was generally regarded, or they might meet an untimely end of their own making like David Koresh.

There can be no argument that Jesus was and remains a great teacher, a change agent, and one who has changed the course of human existence like few who have come before him or after him. But is he the son of God? Are some of the stories attributed to him as wild as the fantasies of some of our modern zealots? You have to decide that for yourself, but there is much to be questioned for me.

What?

What is religion? It is the belief in something or someone, which can vary from casual to fervent. It can also be a belief in nothing. Even non-believers believe in something if nothing more than the conviction that they have uncovered or defrocked the myth that they think is behind religion.

Non-believers believe in something they cannot prove, and their belief is just as valid as the believers who travel through life without proof. Try to explain your position on religion, no matter what it might be, without using the word believe, or explaining what you think. We all rely on a combination of what we've read, heard, and want to think. The Catch-22 is that believing something doesn't make it accurate or fact.

As children, we believe in Santa Claus, the Easter Bunny, and all manner of fairies, goblins, and witches. As we grow older, we think we will be movie stars, professional athletes, the President of the United States, or any number of visions we fervently want to come true.

But believing in something or wishing for something does not make it come true or become a fact or a reality. That is where the word faith comes in.

As humans, we have always wanted and still want to believe in the miracles of religious tales. Yet, there is no proof, save the ravings of some elderly men almost two thousand years ago, and no way to prove or disprove those stories without the benefit of modern videos.

Notwithstanding the occasional stain on a driveway or the side of a barn in Florida that everyone believes to be the image of Jesus or Mary, no documented miracle exists since technology allowed us to record such events. Hell, we can't even prove that Bigfoot or flying saucers are real, and we have some somewhat shaky images of that crap.

No one can prove or disprove the existence of a god of thunder called Thor, either. And there is no way to prove or disprove that the God people worship today is reality. We can only have faith that what we believe does or does not exist.

Is religion, as Karl Marx suggested, "the opiate of the people"? We can say there is ample evidence, at least circumstantial evidence, to make a good argument for Marx's conclusion. Some people can be so overcome with the intensity of their faith that they often act as if they were on drugs.

We see examples throughout history where religious zealots have singled out individuals and entire groups of people, labeled them as heretics, witches, warlocks, and infidels, all manner of designations in their drug-like state of mind, to discriminate, at a minimum, and maim and murder in the extreme, those who disagreed with them. Or, as leaders, they empowered and encouraged others to strike these people down and then go to bed at night, convinced they were doing their God's work.

This behavior has parallels with modern times when people high on crack or methamphetamine appear to lose all sense of humanity, their moral compass spinning like an unbalanced top, as they violate every rule defined by either religion or civil law and indiscriminately break laws and kill people.

The human mind, once warped by drugs or ideology, can jettison all vestiges of civilized behavior and a sense of deportment. The user moves into a world no one else, not in the same state of mind, can inhabit or fathom. Whether chemically induced or psychologically induced, it is a form of insanity.

To be clear, I am not labeling those who embrace their beliefs as insane, not as long as they can control their behavior in the face of differing opinions and have not sworn an oath to convert the world to believe as they do at all costs, as the Europeans did upon discovering the New World.

Nor am I suggesting that everyone who attends the services of their chosen religion represents the extreme, lunatic fringes of whatever philosophy they embrace, be it Christianity, Islam, Judaism, Hinduism, or any other following.

If the radicals within one of these groups are in the minority, the majority must step up and clean their own houses. Without that action, all one can conclude is that they concur with the actions of the lunatics.

The evidence is indisputable that some people, for whatever reason, lose their senses and become so mesmerized, so infected with a particular point of view, often evil, that they lose contact with reality. The reality that most people accept as a logical and moderate approach to running a society becomes invisible to the zealot.

There are unquestionably pockets of intense fundamentalism all over the world. After the events of 9/11 in New York City and other targets in the United States, the word fundamentalist brought to mind the image of a Muslim, complete with a kaffiyeh, a long beard, and an assault weapon nestled in their hands. But the executioners of 9/11 represent a minority of the Islamic world.

The truth is that fundamentalism exists in every religion. In Judaism, the Orthodox Jews cleave to the old beliefs and ways and have shown little compunction in punishing those who reject their beliefs. Their attacks on Palestinians are legion, and in 2023 and 2024 approached the inhumanity the Jews themselves suffered under the Nazis.

In the United States, we have had evangelist ministries like Pat Robertson, who would have made you believe God speaks directly to him. In the 1980s, there was a religious zealot named Frank Schaeffer. His boogeyman was abortion. He wrote something he called a Christian Manifesto. An excerpt from that Mein Kampf-like document reads like this:

"There does come a time when force, even physical force, is appropriate... A true Christian in Hitler's Germany and the occupied countries should have defied the false and counterfeit state. This brings us to a current issue that is crucial for the future of the church in the United States: the issue of abortion... It is time we consciously realize that when any office commands what is contrary to God's law, it abrogates its authority. And our loyalty to the God who gave this law then requires that we make the appropriate response in that situation..."

This is the American version of jihad. Schaeffer equated the government of the United States, including our Supreme Court, which declared abortion legal under our constitution, with Hitler and his plan to cleanse the world of Jews. He is placing his God's laws above the Constitution of the United States.

According to Schaeffer, if the government takes actions that are in opposition to what you believe, as a Christian, Buddhist, Jew, or Muslim, you are entitled to feel, nay empowered by God to overthrow the government and institute religious law in place of civil law.

We have to wonder how many of the people who killed or tried to kill doctors who were providing this critical medical service to their patients were followers of Schaeffer and others like him.

The fact that the laws in this country and others about abortion were, and still are, viewed as a civil right by all, including the Supreme Court of the United States, means nothing to the people on the extreme right.

They are so incensed, so addled by the drug effect of their philosophy, that they can lower all barriers to civilized behavior in pursuit of their myopic dogma.

It's true that the SCOTUS kicked a woman's right to decide to be a mother or not to the curb when they tossed it back to the states, knowing full well that a significant number of states would try to outlaw abortion. They didn't outlaw it, but they might as well have. That's our next great battle for democracy, reestablishing a woman's right to not be a mother and not have a bunch of conservative men force her to be one against her will.

So, there you have it. This is an argument for a theocracy that exists in other parts of the world and was explicitly singled out by the founding fathers as a danger to our freedom. Our founders spoke to the dangers of religious law staining civil law, as has happened with the SCOTUS ruling.

Jefferson wrote: Believing with you that religion is a matter which lies solely between a man and his God, that he owes account to none other for his faith or his worship, that the legislative powers of government reach actions only and not opinions, I contemplate with sovereign reverence that act of the whole American people which declared that their legislature should 'make no law respecting an establishment of religion, or prohibiting the free exercise thereof,' thus building a wall of separation between Church and State.

Madison wrote: The settled opinion here is that religion is essentially distinct from Civil Government and exempt from its cognizance; that a connection between them is injurious to both; that there are causes in the human breast, which ensure the perpetuity of religion without the aid of the law; that rival sects, with equal rights, exercise mutual censorship in favor of good morals;

Madison again: The experience of the United States is a happy disproof of the error so long rooted in the unenlightened minds of well-meaning Christians, as well as in the corrupt hearts of persecuting usurpers, that without a legal incorporation of religious and civil polity, neither could be supported. A mutual independence is found most friendly to practical religion, to social harmony, and to political prosperity.

Let's take a short break from all this old English speech. The word civilization is based on the word civil, which are the laws that we call civil laws.

Is it legal to incite people to acts of violence based on your personal beliefs? That argument has been going on since the birth of democracy. Where does freedom of speech end and insurrection begin?

We know that it is against the law for a citizen to advocate for the killing of our President or any elected member of government. What if they call for the killing of non-government citizens?

In Chaplinsky v. New Hampshire, the court ruled, "There are certain well-defined and narrowly limited classes of speech, the prevention and punishment of which have never been thought to raise constitutional problems."

There are multiple examples of this kind of extremism in our country and countries all over the world. I won't bore you with more examples, but if you would like to know more, there is a wealth of information on the Internet. Just Google something like "extreme religious beliefs around the world." Be prepared to be afraid, very afraid.

It may be time to interject a remark about the Internet. I'm not sure that any technological advance in the history of civilization has had the power of the Internet to affect the future of humans on this planet, both positively and negatively. And that is no small statement in light of some of the medical and technological advances humans have made.

If you, like me, are an Internet junkie, be responsible. Don't take the first argument, statement, or site that supports what you want to believe as gospel and start blasting it all over the web; that includes what I'm writing and saying. Take the time to vet information. Find at least two more respectable sources to corroborate the info, preferably four out of five if you're dealing with a touchy topic.

Don't be a doofus and parrot everything you find online to make a point. In this age of instant communication, where we can reach thousands and sometimes millions of people with our opinions and blather, we have all become journalists, editors, and publishers, and we are obligated not to pass on false, misleading, or inflammatory information.

We have access to every institution of higher learning in the world. We don't have to take the word of some blogger we've never heard of and repeat their nonsense around the world like it was, well, the gospel.

Back to our discussion of religion and what it represents. Regardless of the fanatics referred to earlier and all the others that are out there preaching fire and brimstone, religion is playing less and less of a role in the lives of many people, if not a majority.

In Italy, arguably the world center for Catholicism, various studies have put regular attendance at mass around 30% over the last decade. Elsewhere in deeply secular Western Europe, the "nones" — those rejecting organized religion — are growing fast. In Italy, long considered the cradle of the Catholic faith, most people retain a nominal affiliation, steeped in tradition but with little adherence to doctrine or practice.

According to the latest Pew Research Center survey, 78% of Italians profess to be Catholic. However, the Italian statistics agency, ISTAT, says only 19% attend services at least weekly, while 31% never attend.

While some may disagree with these statistics, the way climate change deniers avoid the truth about our planet, everything, including religion, evolves. People, animals, plants, societies, and institutions evolve, or they die — become extinct.

Religion is evolving, notwithstanding the pockets of fundamentalism that persist. That resistance to change could very well mean they are slated for extinction, and that will almost certainly lead to more and more denial and, probably, violence.

Look at the more progressive churches and religious groups that have opened their theological doors to women in the clergy, accepting the gay and lesbian community into their churches and accepting various social changes that were considered heretical less than one hundred years ago.

The fundamentalists, on the other hand, not only resist change and modernity within their groups, but in numerous instances, they grow angry, resort to discrimination, isolation, and violence, and seem determined to persuade the world to embrace the ideology of the Dark Ages rather than move forward with the rest of the world.

I see this as a kind of social death dance, the writhing that an animal or person might go through when they know that they are dying. While helpless to stop the process, they will try anything they can to cling to life. Like a snake that has lost its head, they will die slowly, but die they must.

Institutions can become irrational, resorting to extreme measures to survive. These actions can take many forms: corporations changing their names after being caught in a scandal, firing CEOs to revitalize stockholders' confidence, blaming the media or their competition for dragging their good name through the mud or introducing radical new product lines. All of these can be drastic actions to try to avoid what appears to be their ultimate demise.

Recently, as you hear this, Donald Trump was convicted on 34 counts of fraud. His immediate reaction was to attack the justice system and demonize the judge, jury, and everyone associated with his conviction. This is what a dying entity does; it strikes out at anyone within striking distance.

Religion has seen the introduction of rock music in church and the move away from Latin mass in the Catholic Church, all in defense of sustaining the institution's life. Changes in dress codes, the liturgy, and even the architecture and interior design of churches are planned to hang on to the dwindling members of their flock and hopefully attract new ones.

Institutions, churches, corporations, and people seldom look inward for the cause of their impending demise. It is human nature to look outward for the exterior cause of a problem. Remember, all these non-human entities (despite the Supreme Court ruling in Citizens United) are nothing more than a collection of like-minded humans acting in concert to advance the interests and well-being of the corporation, church, or institution of any stripe; it is a form of self-preservation. We all tend to find others to blame for our failings.

A similar yet unique evolution has occurred in Eastern religions like Hinduism, Jainism, Sikhism, Taoism, Shinto, Confucianism, and Buddhism mentioned above. While evolving in their own right, many still embrace multiple deities. But they are all being forced to address the sexism, racism, and other biases that have defined their faith.

I am convinced that the violent and debased acts of religious extremists have a similar root cause, if more personal and complicated. Extremism, existing in all religions, is an ideology far removed from the mainstream of society, as well as many members of their faith. They conflict with accepted moral standards in modern society.

I also think that, despite their enthusiasm and commitment, extremists know they are on the lunatic fringes of society. They feel ostracized, which only fuels their anger that the rest of the world doesn't see what they think they see so clearly.

Much like the mentally ill, they may have moments of lucid thought when they realize that it is only those who share their disturbed world who accept and understand them. The rest of the world considers them unbalanced, and justifiably so. When 'you are in a crowd of one hundred people, and the speaker asks everyone who believes in Bigfoot to raise their hand, if you're the only one who does, it begins to dawn on you that you are an outlier. You have two options. Reexamine your beliefs, or withdraw and become an extremist, probably an angry one.

Religious zealots, as a rule, are a collective of like-minded individuals who refuse to look at and adapt to a changing world, and they all face similar issues. The number of adherents may begin to shrink. They hear whisperings about their antiquated beliefs, or even worse, the press starts to show the world that this or that religious faction is a dangerous "collection of weirdos." They begin to withdraw from the mainstream, circling the wagons, as it were, to prevent their extinction.

This is a form of institutional schizophrenia. If I substitute the word institution for people in a definition of schizophrenia, we get: "Schizophrenia is a serious mental health condition that affects how institutions think, feel, and behave. It may result in a mix of hallucinations, delusions, and disorganized thinking and behavior. Hallucinations involve seeing things or hearing voices that aren't observed by others. Delusions involve firm beliefs about things that are not true. Institutions with schizophrenia can seem to lose touch with reality, which can make daily living very hard." Thanks to the Mayo Clinic for that definition.

Religions or churches are less likely to start "cleaning house" as corporations might do. They refuse to accept responsibility for their decline, preferring to blame the media, video games, various music genres, movies, and a general decline of morality in society instead of the waning appeal of their message. They remain steadfast in their conviction that only they know God's plans for humankind and our planet.

All institutions can suffer from the same affliction — rigor mortis, thinking — rigor meaning stiffness, and mortis meaning death. They are consumed with a rigidity of thought and have a death grip, literally, on an obsolete model of human life and behavior from a time when all other artifacts of that era are buried under layers and layers of sediment, progress, and human enlightenment. Everything from those bygone days, except their ideology, resides in museums. It's part of our history, but not relevant to the present.

These groups are much like a herd of animals whose food supply has been devastated by drought or pestilence. They refuse to move due to ignorance or stubbornness. Like those animals, these institutions will die in their tracks or run stampeding over a cliff like so many wildebeest.

Religion, as we have come to think of it, is already in its final days. Final days can mean another century, two centuries, or more. This is not to say the world will embrace agnosticism or atheism, though both belief systems will grow exponentially.

Many people will hang on to the mainstream religions that find a harmony of partnership with science and the realities of the surrounding universe. Let me hasten to say I am not referring to

Scientology as a mainstream belief; it's as wayward a philosophy as any I have heard.

I have said that humans, at this point in our evolution, both socially and psychologically, continue to need the belief in a higher power that they believe is orchestrating a predetermined existence rather than one of randomness. We continue to fear the unknown and the randomness of life. Our logical brains are still not controlling our emotions

Eventually, a majority will accept that order comes not from a mysterious entity like a god but from common-sense civil laws and the logical conduct of human behavior in society. They will also accept the power of a universe that remains in a constant state of motion and evolution, driven by the forces of physics and energies, many of which we are still trying to fathom.

As we come to understand our world, our universe, and ourselves, our fears of a world falling into lawlessness and decline without the torch of religious morality to guide us will be replaced with the knowledge and understanding that humans, like all other elements in our universe, must play by the rules of nature and physics to survive.

It might be seen as the human laws of physics, the rules that dictate our survival in an ever-increasing mass of humanity on our planet. And who knows what other cultures might exist in the universe to complicate the equation? What might they believe?

Another quick aside: I have begun to change my opinion about the probability of intelligent or sentient life on another planet. Looking at the immensity of the universe and the millions or billions of elements that had to come together on Earth to support human life, it seems increasingly unlikely to me that such an occurrence is common throughout the universe. It's not impossible, but as we learn more about our universe, the odds are against many such planets existing.

Of course, unless we or another species can overcome the problem of traveling light years in the blink of an eye to visit other galaxies, the odds are pretty long that we'll ever find each other. It's more likely that the next generations, perhaps a dozen generations, of telescopes like the Webb Space Telescope will allow us to see in finite detail what's out there but not physically visit these places.

Okay, back on topic. There will still be a kind of religion, a philosophy that embraces human morality. This new philosophy will ensure that, unlike many churches in history, we will continue to learn, grow, and adapt to the world around us.

How can we define what religion is? Religion, which can look like mass hysteria at times, is a very personal experience. Everyone has in their mind their temple, chapel, mosque, or cathedral, where they can go any time of the day or night to find comfort and solace from a tormenting world.

In the generic sense of philosophy, religion is what you want it to be. It is the world in which you want to live, free from whatever demons lurk in the dark regions of your imagination. But there is a line or limit—a fence, if you will—that needs to be drawn in your mind.

You have every right to feel as you do, but you have no right to impose that world on others. I have said to friends in discussions on religion that you have every right to dance naked around a boulder in the moonlight if you believe that will bring you peace and please your deity, but you cannot and must not try to force me to do the same; that will only bring you pain and grief when I refuse. Not to mention that no one wants to see me naked or dancing.

When?

When did this all happen? Evolution is a slow process, so it would seem that it is not a matter of "when" so much as a series of whens linked together over quite an extended period. That sounds like evolution to me. Yes, I know there is no such words as whens, but it's my book and my dictionary.

Admittedly, among some of the simpler species, evolution can happen in a couple of generations, but given their short lifespans, I suspect evolution still represents a significant period for them. In their universe, from birth to death, whether five days or 100 years, it is still a lifetime. What I don't know is if they have any concept of time.

As discussed earlier, archeological evidence indicates that humans have had rituals that revolved around fertility, birth, and death, reaching back tens of thousands of years, long before Christ, Buddha, Mohammed, or any other person generally linked to one religion or another joined the parade of religious leaders and prophets across the millennia, offering their version and vision of the reason for the existence of the world and humans.

Might there have been religious or philosophical leaders and teachers long before recorded history? (Recorded history includes finding graves and other artifacts to establish our journey.) Possibly. But to this point, we've not seen anything.

Religious beliefs have morphed over the millennia from the notion of multiple gods, each controlling various aspects of human life, to a single all-powerful god, at least in the Western world. Over time, people likely became dissatisfied with the religion of the day and branched out, evolving their versions of how the world began, who was in charge, and, of course, why you should listen to them and not the other guys.

To confound the picture further, many religions have similar legends about events like the Great Flood, suggesting to me that they were at least exposed to stories of other religions, perhaps by traveling storytellers, merchants, or missionaries.

Those exposed to these new stories then cherry-picked the parts they thought worthy of their philosophy, adding the names of people from their part of the world and blending it all with their culture, while rejecting the stories they found unworthy of their beliefs and pronouncements. Europeans' forced religion on the indigenous peoples of the Americas is a perfect example of how Catholic rituals were blended with indigenous beliefs and festivals to give us the Latin version of Christianity.

It might be noted here that while mainstream Christianity, Judaism, and Islam worship a single god, the same God, interpretations of His message are all over the place, like a dog's breakfast. Several holy individuals remain in Christianity who, though not as revered as God, are nevertheless considered icons for a number of religions. These include the Virgin Mary and numerous saints to whom people often pray.

Interestingly, to me, Judaism and Islam, decidedly intense adversaries, share the belief that Jesus was not the son of God but possibly a prophet (Islam), and I assume neither religion considers his mother to be anything more than his mother.

Christian Orthodox religions often rely on icons of saints as a conduit to God. Although they accept most of the precepts of other Christian sects, their rituals are noticeably different.

In many European countries, towns hold weekly festivals in honor of a saint or deity they have adopted as their patron saint. My wife, Gale, gave me a book some years ago that took you to a different festival every week throughout the year in Italy. This is a vacation I would enjoy beyond imagination for the food, wine, festivities, and, yes, the colorful religious celebrations.

My personal beliefs notwithstanding, religion has delivered some beautiful, if at times bizarre, traditions, as well as unbelievable mosques, temples, and cathedrals. While I do not subscribe to any religion, as a lover of art and architecture, I cannot help but be amazed and impressed. People's passion for their faith drove them to create incredible structures and works of art they no doubt believed would please God. At the same time, some of them simultaneously rejected idols. As they say, there can be some good and bad in everything.

Judaism and Islam have no extra deities that I know of. However, they greatly respect people like Mohammed, Abraham, Moses, and Jesus. In Islam, Mohammed is held in such high esteem that no one is supposed to try to draw his likeness, let alone question his deity or compare him to anyone else. This doctrine seems to have the Old Testament's underpinning: "Thou shalt have no other Gods before "me. "Those who have dared to produce images of Mohammed are in danger of suffering some of that Old Testament retribution that appears to be a significant part of Islamic philosophy.

The beginnings of the Christian religion, as practiced by most of the Western world, were focused on Africa and the Middle East around the time of Christ or shortly after that, followed by offshoots of those religions within the last 500 to 1,000 years. Of course, Judaism flourished well before the Christian era, but that religion is experiencing its own evolution, such as Jews for Jesus.

Before the emergence of the various major religions, those preceding the rise of Jesus, there had been a multitude of social experiments in the world regarding religion or spirituality of one kind or another.

I mentioned earlier how some people espoused the single-god theory long before it became popular. The pharaohs and emperors claimed they were gods or descendants of the gods. There had to have been other fringe and perhaps odd beliefs that were born and died long before we started writing down what we were thinking and doing. All that is forever lost to the dustbin of unrecorded history unless someone makes an extraordinary discovery buried in a cave.

Today, the three dominant religions in the Western world, or at least those with the most adherents, including Eastern Europe and Africa, recognize Africa, the Middle East, and Jerusalem as the birthplace of Christianity, Islam, and Judaism. All three religions look at and claim Jerusalem as the center of their faith and claim that city as their own. The sad thing about this situation is that some of these devoutly religious people see no problem with engaging in violence in pursuit of winning their argument.

I should probably state here or reiterate that for the sake of simplicity, I am lumping Catholics, Protestants, and Orthodoxy under the general heading of Christianity. You will have to deal with that.

I said I would focus on Western philosophies, but I should mention that Hinduism is no small potato on the religious map of humanity. With a polytheistic and ritual tradition comprising numerous cults and sects, Hinduism is the oldest of several religions in South Asia. It is a unifying force of Indian culture and the social caste system. Much of the rest of Asia is dominated by Islam and Buddhism, with a smattering of Christianity and a few local beliefs.

The holy city of Mecca, as well as Jerusalem, plays a major role in Islam as the birthplace of Mohammed. Mecca is the destination for millions of Muslim pilgrims every year on a quest called the Hajj. Likewise, Jews and Christians make pilgrimages to Jerusalem to visit the holy sites that are at the center of their faith.

I have postulated that most religions—I call them new religions because they were once new—were offshoots of what came before. Disaffected followers of the old religion broke away, modified what was being taught, and began their new religion.

Were we seeking better answers? Did our evolving knowledge of our world and society cause us to look at the older religions and myths with doubt? I suspect it is a little of all those things and much more.

Jesus was a Jew who found the behavior of Jewish religious leaders and their unlikely partnerships with the Roman Empire unsavory, if not deplorable. He revolted against the corrupted and politically entwined religion of Judaism and went about preaching a new doctrine that emphasized honesty, integrity, and, at a minimum, empathy for your fellow man, if not outright love.

It was this philosophy that would become the basis of Christianity and, of course, cost Jesus his life. Today, many of his followers seem to have forgotten his message of peace, tolerance, and love. Just as many Muslims have also forgotten Mohammed's messages, carrying the same theme. They have never heard this doctrine in their mosque, synagogue, or church or chose to ignore it. More than a few individuals in all religions have chosen to twist the teachings to their own warped, misleading, selfish, or devious ends.

Islam likely found its roots in the disappointment the people of the time felt in what they must have seen as the contradictions in the teachings and behaviors of both the Christians and the Jews. Islam is, it seems to me, a blend of what Jesus taught and the Old Testament, which is full of violence and retribution rather than forgiveness.

Many religious zealots are like the political conservatives in modern times who pontificate about morality and family values, only to be featured in the evening news for having wandered away from their supposed convictions. The rumors persist of Muslim men sneaking off to the UAE to party. To falter is to be human, no matter your beliefs.

Wanting some of the conservatism of the more orthodox Judaism, as found in the Old Testament, as well as evolving conservative ideas of their own, and like the Jews rejecting Jesus as the son of God, Muslims spun off their own religion while still respecting Jesus as a prophet.

This pattern of discontent with the current religious dogma has continued for over 2,000 years as church after church has broken away from one main church branch or another to rewrite, or at least proffer their interpretation of the Bible, Torah, or Quran, and what they believe is God's message to anyone who will listen.

One thing we do know is that humans are curious. Unlike a cow, a horse, or any number of animals that appear to be satisfied with their lot in life, humans keep looking for something new, something different, and something we believe will be better than what we will be leaving behind if we move on, whether in this life or what, we hope, will be the next life. We question the status quo with a passion, challenge authority, and change tradition. This has been problematic for many religions that steadfastly and stubbornly hold on to the old beliefs and old ways.

That tendency to resist change continues today as statistics show more and more people are moving away from the older tenets of religion. A recent poll indicates that fewer than six of ten people worldwide identify as religious. With some over eight billion of us on the planet, that means that something approaching five billion people have turned their backs on religion, or at least as it is taught. With a few exceptions, even fewer of us attend services regularly.

Are we abandoning religion? Has religion abandoned us? Or is religion morphing once again into something that fits a modern world where science will provide the explanations for many of the heretofore mysteries of life that were claimed by religion?

I have no doubt that we are seeing the continuation of religious evolution, which may well mean the end of religion as we know it at some point in the future, much the same way that the multiple god theory faded into history. This prophecy can drive the fundamentalists to distraction or even acts of violence, as we have seen when topics like gay marriage and abortion are debated in society.

As I write this, the United States has experienced a sea change in public opinion regarding gay marriage. Even the new Pope, Francis, preaches tolerance and acceptance toward the LGBT community. However, he refuses to allow gay priests, which is ironic and a bit humorous.

Although Pope Francis has passed the test of time, I continue to worry about him. Castle politics and intrigue are alive and well in any institution, and given his approach to challenging dogma, he could end up having a mysterious illness. But he is aging rapidly, so we may be watching the Vatican chimney again one of these days.

Regardless of how the fundamentalists resist change, it will happen; it always has. As I type this, in 2024, our conservative Supreme Court ruled that it is unconstitutional for any state to deny a marriage license to same-sex couples. Now tell me that is not religious evolution, given the makeup of the current Court. It is now on the churches to find a way to come to grips with a civil law that they can apply to all of their followers.

To those who resist, it must appear the world has gone to hell in a handbasket, but that has been the position of most religions toward any progressive movement since the beginning of time. There was a time when almost no one chose their life partner in much of the world. Their marriages were arranged by their parents. Religion saw no problem with that approach and, in fact, participated in the process. That practice persists today in some countries, but like many of the old ideas, it is in its waning moments.

Catholics didn't marry non-Catholics, and Jews only married Jews. It was illegal in parts of our country for Black and White people to marry. For centuries, religions condoned slavery. Virtually all these now archaic practices were mourned by religion when society decided it was time to change. I can't predict what new changes will occur, but they will undeniably change. Consider, for instance, the austere beginnings of many of the churches in the United States at the beginning.

While ostensibly seeking freedom of religion and shedding the yokes of the Church of England's rather harsh edicts and class-ruled society, religious orders in the new United States, like the Puritans and Quakers, tried to force everyone in their area of influence to worship and believe as they did, even to the extent of persecution and imprisonment. That sounds similar to what they fled in England. And it continues to be a concern as a fundamentalist minority in our government pushes to make religious laws the law of the land.

There were townships in the United States that passed laws requiring citizens to attend services on Sundays. And, of course, there were laws forbidding any number of activities on Sunday, including having a drink.

These kinds of rules were legion. This is what they called freedom of religion. It was closer to the strict laws of Sharia than to the freedoms our founders sought to establish. It was only free if you followed the dictates of your particular pastor. Moving to another town could easily change the rules.

But other groups, religious and non-religious alike, resisted this conservative message and the idea of having a state religion embedded in our constitution, opting instead for a separation of church and state in our government. These people had seen in Europe what could happen when the government and the church became bedfellows. Some of the founding fathers of the United States, including Thomas Jefferson, were Deists.

Deism is defined by dictionary.com" as:

> "A belief in the existence of a God on the evidence of reason and nature only, with the rejection of supernatural revelation (distinguished from theism). And, a belief in a God who created the world but has since remained indifferent to it."

Theism contends there is a God and that humans and the world are the work of His creation. For them, there is no alternative.

Though well documented, religious zealots, some holding elective office, argue against the separation of church and state to move us toward a more theocratic form of government. But whose version of religion would that be?

If we are to move toward a theocracy, which religion should rule the day in terms of our morality and laws? Will it be Christianity, Judaism, Islam, Buddhism, or some other religion? According to the Pew Research folks, we have at least 14 beliefs, including Christian and non-Christian, non-affiliated and non-believers.

Obviously, the vocal religious conservatives presently are mostly, if not all, Christians of various stripes. We should keep in mind the pain and suffering inflicted on people during the Inquisition and the Crusades in the name of Christian beliefs before we side with these folks or anyone else promoting a theocratic form of government. I, personally, find little difference between the extreme Christian zealots and those in favor of Sharia law.

History has shown that with a theocracy, it goes badly for just about everyone except those at the head of the church. Who is to say that there won't be a Jewish majority or president in our lifetime? Or a Muslim or Buddhist? Will we all go along with their version of morality and religion? Will we be willing to follow their religious laws?

Our own short history in the United States has seen us move from churches where men and women sat on opposite sides of the church, periods where we believed some people to be possessed by demons, and times when we drowned or burned witches at that stake, to a more open and free society.

We have become decidedly more liberal in our approach to worship. We now have modern churches where rock groups play music as part of the services. Are we ready to let those who would take us backward a hundred years or more, enforcing a much more conservative approach to American life, roll back the changes we have made as a civilized society? Let alone impose religious laws on our everyday behavior.

The floundering Mars Hill Church in Seattle, whose leader resigned, apparently due to problems of his own making, is an example of this religious evolution at work. Starting in 1996, the church spread to four states in the Northwest. Dodging a lawsuit accusing him of misappropriating $30 million worth of members' tithes, Driscoll moved to Scottsdale, Arizona., to start a new church in 2016 called Trinity Church. In 2021, he once again faced similar allegations from former followers.

Does this represent the future of religion in the United States? Not the skulduggery, but the populist approach to religion? Is it better or worse than any other church? I don't think so; it is just different. It's a church trying to appeal to modern, youthful spiritual, emotional, and psychological needs. Along with this new approach comes all the corruption that has plagued most religious institutions throughout history.

Those who lead any institution, government, religion, or corporation have to be aware of what the public and their target audience want and find a way to deliver that. That is what marketing is all about. Whether you are selling laundry detergent or religion, you must know your audience and have your finger on the pulse of public opinion.

Oh, and understand that these days, with smartphones, computers, and access to the Internet, all the world is the media. Be sure you have nothing to hide if you aspire to be a public figure. Don't try to sell anyone snake oil.

To further demonstrate what I am saying and with a nod to the speed of change, in 2015, Episcopalians elected their first-ever Black presiding Bishop, Bishop Michael Curry. That comes on the heels of them electing their first female bishop—that is lightning in a bottle in terms of evolution, especially social evolution.

What is the conclusion we can draw from the question, When? When did religion begin? The question isn't when, but rather the reality that when is now and has been since the beginnings of organized religion. Every new religion at the time it emerged or morphed from a previous philosophy, whether five years ago or 5000 years ago, was the religion of now at that time.

When a religion meets people's needs for the current time, conditions, and culture, its followers are content. When the church seems to have lost touch with a changing world, holding tenuously to an antiquated past, its followers will seek new answers.

As the world and all of its cultures change, along with our understanding of the universe we live in, religion will need to change with it, even if that means giving way to another philosophy. I think Pope Francis gets that to a degree. It's either change or become a footnote in history, as so many institutions have done over time. I once read an inspiring saying that said something to the effect, "Good things come to those who wait, but it's only the things left behind by those on the move."

Our world and all the societies in it are on the move and have been throughout history. As a species, we are destined and perhaps driven to be on the move. Those who cling stubbornly to the old religious or political ways are destined to become a dwindling minority and then fade into obsolescence.

I am well aware that I have repeated that message a few times here, but it is an important message that goes to the heart of this essay. Let me interject with something I heard at a symposium on technological evolution many years ago when I worked for Boeing.

The speaker, whose name is lost to the dustbins of my memory, used the example of computers (what we had back then is archaic today) and how we moved from radio vacuum tubes (look that up if you're under about 50 or 60 years old) to modern computers. His presentation focused on companies that don't evolve with the times, but the model is true for just about everything pertaining to the human experience.

He presented to our group a hypothetical company, let's call it Applesoft (I couldn't resist that), that had invented the transistor to replace the vacuum tube — in reality, that was Bell Laboratories in 1947.

In this hypothetical company, Applesoft, sales boomed. They had revolutionized the radio industry. They made millions from their invention. But they stopped evolving and innovating.

While they sat back, raked in the profits, and paid dividends to their euphoric stockholders, other companies and the competition were busy improving Applesoft'soft's invention. This work led to the integrated circuit and then the Intel chip that powers computers in the modern world.

Today, we have smartwatches with computing power that used to require a machine the size of a walk-in refrigerator. By the time a company realizes it is being overtaken, it's too late. The speaker called this artistic obsolescence: sitting back and admiring what you've done while others look for the next generation of technology. Good things come to those who wait, but only what is left over by those on the move.

Why is religion so reticent to change? Because those men in the powerful position of religious leadership don't want to concede their power to another group or belief system, any more than those long-ago warriors were willing to step aside when some brainiac in the tribe suggested some invisible warriors were mightier than them.

Combine that with the conviction that virtually every word in the Bible was spoken by God to one holy man or another at some point in history. A God who is infallible, invisible, can't ever be wrong. You are not likely to sway the thinking of the religious zealot. You may piss him off, but you are not likely to break through that wall of indoctrination.

Like the technology company, they are convinced that they have arrived at the ultimate understanding of the universe and life. And while they bask in the light of their presumed knowledge, science continues to find new answers.

When we become rich, powerful, or famous, we can become isolated from reality and, at times, complacent, basking in the glory of our greatness, not unlike a team that has won the Super Bowl or World Series. A letdown can set in after we have "achieved our goal. We think we have arrived; we are the ultimate. That is a dangerous place to be in any endeavor or relationship.

Religious philosophy must evolve, constantly reexamining and reinventing itself while maintaining its core competencies. Otherwise, it risks becoming artistically obsolete and ending up existing only in the corners of museums around the world, where people of the future will visit and wonder what our world was like. They will wonder why these people stood still, allowing themselves to fade into history.

Where Did This All Begin?

Where did religion begin? In my humble opinion, and by now you have heard how humble I can be, religion occurred in many places at about the same time, which I don't find surprising. I will explain that comment a bit further along.

Since many religions do not salute the same deities, I find it difficult to accept any argument that purports that some sort of global epiphany attributable to a single god or event gave birth to religion worldwide. There was no Shazam! No puff of white smoke, flash of light, intellectual or theocratic big bang. There was no waving of a magic wand that suddenly produced our world, the universe, and all it contains or that drove humans to be consumed by the desire to pray.

It seems more likely to me to be associated with human evolution from animals into what we today call humans. As we evolved, and more specifically as our brains began to develop beyond the simple act of eating, sleeping, pooping, and procreating like some beast in a pasture, a higher form of reasoning and logic emerged in the way we perceived and interacted with both the world around us, with other human beings, and with the many mysteries of life.

We were no longer primates driven by instinct. We had developed the ability to wonder who we were, why we were, where we might have come from, where we will go next, and what the world around us means.

You often hear that animals, typically, have no sense or awareness of self. If most animals are put in front of a mirror, they will ignore their own image — it has no meaning to them. Put a human or many primates in front of a mirror, and the result is strikingly different. Yes, a few other animals appear to be sentient, but more discovery is needed.

Even more interesting to me is my belief that religion happened in more than one place, more or less simultaneously. In archeological terms, we may be speaking of a period of 10,000 years or more. Evolution is not a flash of light.

In places as far removed from each other as Africa and China, Judaism in Africa, and Hinduism in India, Confucianism in China, religion has become a human need. The question of the human need to believe in something would seem indisputable.

While I'm not ready to call religion a drug, it did seem to fill a human need and appears to have an addictive, enchanting, or mesmerizing quality. But then, more innocuous pastimes such as professional football and video games fill a similar need. Apparently, there are centers of our brain that need stimulation.

There can be no question that as we migrated across continents, we interacted with other tribes either socially, as conquerors, or at other times as the conquered ones fleeing to another place. These migrations meant that we shared or were forced to share the beliefs of different groups, effectively homogenizing tradition and religion.

The migrants and explorers from, let us say, India did not arrive in Africa to find a country devoid of any belief or philosophy. The Indians, arriving in Africa, probably brought their culture and beliefs with them. If they arrived in conquest, then one group either suggested or tried to force another to abandon their long-held beliefs and adopt a new one, typically that of the conquerors.

The resistance to such change is understandable, but evolution, like death and taxes, is inevitable. You might resist change for a time, but it will happen. Yet, in most forms of evolution, be it physical or social, it appears that the old guard does not go down without a fight. There is often a struggle to the death, literally or figuratively, to try to live on as we always have. The death throes associated with such social change parallels what all living creatures experience in the end.

Another observation that I will present as evidence of what I am putting forth goes back to the previous paragraph, where I wrote, "one group either suggesting or trying by force. . ." Force is the operable word in that statement. Try to recall a time in history when conquerors tried to gently persuade the conquered into accepting their social norms or selling their ideas like laundry soap. If such instances exist at all, they would be few and far between.

Something in the human psyche, once convinced we are right, or worse, that we are the chosen ones, sends us into a frenzy of evangelism to change the world. In that frenzy, there are no holds barred in our zeal to convert the masses. I won't offer a history lesson here. Still, I am confident you can find all manner of examples of this nonsense in history.

One last remark about violence. While the current focus in most of the world right now is on the crazies who are giving Islam a bad name, they have no corner on the market for insanity and brutality. Just about every major religion in history has behaved in a like manner at one time or another.

Back to the subject of this book. Let's look at an opposable thumb as an example of the phenomenon called evolution. That anatomical change appears to have happened in primates of multiple species in far-flung regions of the world, not just in one animal in a sudden instant, who then passed the feature on to its offspring. This new feature then would have gone on around the globe, one species at a time, until millions of diverse animals, mostly primates, all had thumbs.

Think about that—how feasible is it that one lonely animal somewhere went to sleep without this critical digit and awoke one morning with a thumb? Then, this lucky creature passed this physical attribute on to its offspring, and they, in turn, passed it on to their offspring until all other animals on the planet eventually had thumbs. We would have had to start that process a couple of billion years earlier than is accepted.

Consider Adam and Eve. What are the odds that the eight billion people living on the earth today, black, white, yellow, brown, fat, skinny, tall, and short, all came from these two naked, most likely dark-skinned, and backward humans living in a garden somewhere in the Middle East, some unknown thousands of years ago?

Many changes must have happened more or less at the same time around the world - again, the same time in terms of evolution might be 10,000 years. Different species of primates in different parts of the world were all developing opposable thumbs simultaneously because evolution created a demand for thumbs. In anthropological terms, this process may have taken hundreds or even thousands of years.

I accept as a fact that all life came from the sea, if for no other reason than the fact that the entire earth was covered by water for a long time. What I can't accept is that a single solitary little fish figured out how to breathe out of the water and how to navigate on solid ground by stiffening its little fins. And then, this lonely little air-breathing fish gave birth to every living creature on earth, whether they walk, fly, or slither about out of the water; that concept strikes me as preposterous.

It seems much more probable to me that several fish, or more likely hundreds and thousands of fish in the waters all over the world where land had appeared, figured this out at about the same time, not intellectually, of course, and walked ashore in Asia, Africa, and North and South America. Even if this happened on the original continent, Pangaea, before it broke up into various continents, it still had to occur in more than one place on the shores of Pangaea.

Suppose we are to accept the myth of Adam and Eve. In that case, we have to talk of many Adams and Eves evolving around the same period in various parts of our planet. Why? Because everything was right for humans to emerge from their primate origins.

There is an explanation for these types of phenomena occurring, more or less simultaneously, far apart from each other. I think it may even have a name, but I'll be damned if I can remember what it is called or find it on the Internet; I remember hearing of this theory many years ago. The theory of dynamic systems is the closest I have seen to what I'm about to say. Being impatient, I finally gave up looking for the name after hours of searching.

The concept behind this theory is that any change in life forms, ecosystems, weather systems, or sociological changes can be predicted to a degree. In fact, everything can be anticipated if you can gather enough stable data to become a kind of Nostradamus and get very close to predicting the future.

Back to the opposable thumb. The earliest primates across the globe at the time, or what may have been their predecessors who were neither quite a fish nor quite a primate, were still much the same biologically. They had legs, arms, or wings — yes, I know primates don't have wings, but their ancestors might have; indulge me. They also had eyes, a heart, lungs, etc. They shared a similar form, lifestyle, and diet across their species. If this is even close to the truth, then by eating all the same foods, they were in danger of becoming extinct because they were all competing for the same food; diversity is necessary for survival.

The world around these creatures was constantly changing. The oceans were receding, revealing dry land. Things started to grow, like trees, grass, and various edible plants.

As their environment changed around them and offered the promise of survival by taking advantage of these new food options, it demanded an evolutionary change to access these new food sources that promised their survival or even their advancement to a higher form of life.

Some critters, like certain butterflies, evolved spots to blend with flowers to avoid predators. Others, like tigers, evolved stripes so they might hide in tall grass and become more efficient predators. Various species began to eat different foods and even each other, which became a typical pattern in the living world.

The world around some of these animals required something else, like a thumb, to survive, to access the available food supply, a food supply that those without thumbs could not eat. Voilà, supply and demand. This food supply demanded that certain animals with a propensity for certain foods evolve a thumb to access the food supply they wanted the most.

They began to change their form to allow for a thumb. Perhaps some incident, such as a drought or a weather catastrophe, wiped out their traditional food supply, which had only required them to graze like cattle. Maybe they were simply taking advantage of what nature was offering.

The fish in the sea needed no thumbs to get to their food, and it made swimming awkward. The birds in the sky, able to fly hundreds of miles to find their food and armed with beaks to break open fruit for the seeds and meat, didn't need thumbs. But primates required thumbs and got them.

The animals in question, some of whom are our ancestors, spent several generations or more surviving on whatever they could find. A food source was available to them, but it required greater dexterity than they had so far been equipped to access. Nature forced this change to ensure their survival. Maybe they needed to hold a stick to fish termites from a mound, strip the bark from trees to get to insects, and peel the skins from difficult-to-eat fruits.

We humans are consumed with finding the missing link. What if there is no missing link? What if these changes were so subtle over thousands of years that we would have to uncover tens of thousands of artifacts and lay them side by side chronologically to learn the mystery of how we evolved to what we consider human? This is something to think about.

I suspect the desire to find that missing link goes to our willingness to believe some higher power stepped in and created humans and all animals. We want to think that this all-powerful deity waved a wand, said abracadabra, and there we were. That would be like looking for the missing link that produced a tiger with stripes. Did that happen in one or two generations, or was the change so gradual over many generations that there is no missing link?

Back to that theory of dynamic systems, I mentioned. This phenomenon of simultaneous events occurring in multiple places is basic. The idea revolves around having all the same forces working on a common element or elements, or animals, the weather, and, of course, people, and in different places. It can be applicable to any living entity capable of reacting to a change in its environment. Given similar circumstances acting on any creature or event, the results will be both predictable and comparable, if not precisely the same in every respect.

A simple way to look at this is to examine baking a cake, obviously not a living creature, but valuable to understanding what I'm talking about. Let's say we want to make a chocolate cake. If you precisely measure all the ingredients down to the microgram and do so identically each time you bake a cake. Use precisely the same grade of flour, chocolate, salt, and all the ingredients in the recipe. Suppose you have the oven set at precisely the same temperature, at the same elevation, and with the same temperature and humidity in the surrounding air. In that case, you will produce an identical cake each time. Change is not random; it is predictable based on the variables that affect a given event or entity.

If you change one or more of these variables, add more or fewer of one or more of the ingredients, increase or decrease the oven temperature, etc., you will still get a chocolate cake. However, it will be noticeably different each time you vary the circumstances. It will be drier, wetter, lighter or darker, more or less dense, or flavorful.

This is the essence of evolution. The outcome is predictable if you can accurately measure the variables in advance. You will know with a good deal of certainty what kind of cake you will end up with. Today, we are dealing with climate change. The outcome is predictable based on what we're doing today, and if we don't change, the end game is predictable.

Change in most living organisms is driven by demand — supply and demand. The demand is brought on by environmental factors such as weather, food supply, predators, and a wide range of other influences. The anteater evolves their long nose, the bat its radar system, and the owl its fantastic hearing and night vision. All of these developments were driven by survival. The demand to access what they needed to survive and thrive in a way other animals cannot drove the evolution of unique capabilities. The species that failed to evolve are most likely extinct today.

The driving factors can be whimsical events. If we paid attention, we would know how human actions have driven climate change over time. President Jimmy Carter tried to warn the nation about the downside of fossil fuels back in the 1970s, but the industry and his political opponents succeeded in convincing the public he was crying that the sky was falling. We did nothing, and now we are facing an even greater crisis. Our near-term decisions will drive predictable results over the next thirty or forty years.

Nature can be an unpredictable agent of change in evolution, but only because we don't yet know how to measure everything or control many of the changes. We are closing in on much of this knowledge, such as how to predict earthquakes. Weather forecasting is nothing more than knowing all the ingredients, studying how they will interact, and then predicting the outcome. We will learn more about predicting earthquakes, volcanos, tornadoes, and tsunamis.

The drive to survive and even thrive triggers physical and social changes in organisms all over the planet to accommodate the change happening around them. We know that over the several hundred years that science has studied life on this planet, we have uncovered evidence to prove evolution to be a fact. We accept that animals have evolved both in physical ways and behaviorally to survive the variables that rule the planet.

Yet, we seem less willing to believe that humans have done the same thing. I think that much of this denial is based on the legend that God created us in his image in this flash of light, or whatever his magic was. Therefore, we conclude that we must have been perfect from day one without needing to evolve. If God is perfect, then it follows that we must be perfect as well. Talk about an ego.

Another example of the world's demands and the species' survival can be found in the fact that almost every animal, insect, fish, or fowl has eyes. There are a few exceptions that have evolved without eyes or with exceedingly poor eyesight. Still, they are in the minority of life on this planet, not counting plant life. Those with poor eyesight have evolved other senses and mechanisms to allow them to compete and survive in the world.

As humans, have we evolved the perfect form, like sharks and alligators that have retained their basic form for millions of years? We are close because we don't seem to have drastically changed our physical stature over many thousands of years.

A caveat is in order at this point. I am talking about physical evolution, not intellectual or social evolution. There are areas in those realms where we have made little progress, which might be the focus of another book. I suspect other people who are better educated and brighter than me have covered that topic.

We humans may be a little larger now because we eat better than eons ago, although we're not much bigger than some of the skeletons they have found. Thanks to modern medicine, we may live longer, but intellectually and socially, we are still a work in progress.

Another quick observation: With technology and even physical evolution, we can keep building on the last generation of whatever was built. Suppose you look at the first computers after the inventors died. Their machines were waiting on a desk for the next generation to come along and pick up where they left off, making improvements and moving technology forward.

With social and intellectual evolution, we have to learn everything all over again with each new generation. We can't leave what we learned on a table and have the next generation pick up where we left off.

Every generation of bears that climb a tree to get honey from a beehive is stung in the process. The cubs are denied the knowledge from the previous generation, even though the mama bear tries to dissuade the little dummies from rummaging around in a bee hive. Every generation of dogs encountering a porcupine or skunk must relearn the lesson their parents know.

We humans are the same. Each new generation has to learn a great deal that is not passed on through genetics. We spend the first one-fifth of our lives in school and falling out of trees, learning the lessons over and over.

Where we might be different is our technology and science. We may someday find a way to pass much of this knowledge on biologically to new generations; that will be something if it happens.

Continuing - evolution demanded eyesight to find food and avoid becoming food. If life on this planet at first consisted of microbes and bacteria, as it now seems, they managed to somehow function without eyesight. That was easier than it is today because they may have been the only living organisms on the planet for a few million years.

As these simple one-celled creatures evolved into more complex mechanisms, their bodies required more to sustain than the microscopic food supply that had maintained life for their minuscule ancestors.

It became necessary to have eyes to see and find food, perhaps claws and/or teeth to eat the food, and so on. Of course, some of these new lifeforms became predators that dined on their cousins who had flunked the evolution test.

Once the world began to cool, this evolutionary step of eyesight was not passed from one species to another but developed across the spectrum of animals. The oceans receded, yielding land masses, and the world became a place that could support life just about as we know it. Fish under the sea, birds in the air, and animals on land all had eyes.

Evolution is everywhere.

Plants also evolve. Naturally, once humanity took up agriculture, we gave Mother Nature a hand. We started hybridizing various plants for our own enjoyment, either for food production or aesthetic reasons, like roses. Some people like to call this "playing God." In reality, all we are doing is improving on evolution, which I have noted is typically relatively slow. But nature was still not crossing corn with wheat. I'm not yet aware of any hybrid of corn and wheat.

Now, we have big Agra playing around with adding genes from other species to enhance products. Is this progress or Frankenstein science? No one really knows, and the debate continues, although it appears to me that the genome is out of the bottle, so we need to manage the process, not try to stop it.

Do we need to monitor what the scientists working for Big Agra are doing? You're damn right, we do. Anytime people are doing something with an eye on profits and share values, you need to keep a very close eye on what they are doing. Mother Nature doesn't have a profit motive. If she did, we'd have to watch her just as closely as we watch Monsanto.

I've talked a good deal about physical evolution and, parallel with that, humans and animals—remember, we were animals back in the day and still are. And we are all still going through social evolution. As we experimented with various forms of tribalism, marriage, nomadic life, village life, political systems, and even housing structures, some ideas succeeded famously, while others crashed and burned.

Some examples of social evolution in animals are the domestication of dogs, cats, cattle, horses, and the list goes on. All of these animals were once wild. They accepted domestication, some better than others, and it could be argued that their lives are better for it in terms of comfort. Those we raise for food may be the exception, but there has yet to be an indication that they understand what we're doing to them. They continue to happily swim, graze, and peck their way through life until the grim reaper descends on them.

Survival generally dictated what change was needed, and those failing to heed the need for change became part of our planet's history. That is the history that sees us now scouring the seas and deserts looking for the evidence of these long-extinct creatures, more evidence of our insatiable desire to understand everything.

It would appear to me that there is no "where" in terms of human evolution, be it physical, social, or religious. It started in many places, in many ways, and generally during the same era, as measured in tens of thousands of years, but it was always driven by the need for the human brain to come to grips with the world around us.

Since this story is in English, it will most likely be heard by English speakers in the Western World. For that reason, I will limit my discussion of the 'Where' to what we think of as Western religions: Christianity, Judaism, and Islam. Islam has come into much of the Western consciousness in the last few decades, even though it has existed for some 1,400 years.

I welcome adherents of Eastern religions to enjoy or debunk my theories. However, I will limit my scope to avoid carrying on for days and weeks on end, and the limitations of my knowledge of many of these philosophies, and my reluctance to do that much work.

These Western religions are all related. As I've said, Christianity spun off from Judaism, and Islam spun off from Christianity and Judaism. That fact alone should be recognized by the antagonists in all three faiths. They are more alike and have more in common than they have differences. All this violence over minor differences is unnecessary.

As I posited earlier, the various religions are the work of disappointed followers of an older school of thought who felt, rightly or wrongly, that they had been disenfranchised by their current religion. They broke away from their church, synagogue, or mosque, found other disenfranchised and like-thinking individuals, and voilà, you had a new sect of a religion, or a totally new religion altogether. If you peel away the layers of the religious onion, there isn't a nickel's worth of difference between any of them. The differences are strictly semantic.

I may have strayed there, but I hope that some of that discussion provides a context for what comes next. We were examining the Where of religion. We Westerners need to be less parochial; we need to rid ourselves of the "not invented here" attitude. Around 10,000 BCE, some of the first cities, states, kingdoms, and religions begin to emerge in the south of India. I'm going to prattle on a bit with historical facts - I hope you will bear with me. I'm not a fan of long lists like this and if you choose to skim or even skip over it, I understand; I thought it germane to my argument.

Four or five wooden posts were erected near the site of modern-day Stonehenge around 8000 BCE; that's about 10,000 years ago. Between 7500 and 5700 BCE, Stonehenge was a probable religious site.

Çatalhöyük, a proto-city settlement in southern Anatolia that existed from approximately 7500 BCE to 6400 BCE and flourished around 7000 BCE, developed in Anatolia in what is modern-day Turkey. For the next 5,000 years, religion continued to spread and evolve and would, in time, influence Europe and the Mediterranean.

This era of religious evolution, among other sometimes bizarre practices, began to embrace the idea of a sacrifice, both animal and human. In the last 3,000 years of religious history, a myriad of events occurred, all of which are at your fingertips if you use a computer. A few of the highlights are offered here:

- Newgrange, the 250,000-ton passage tomb in Ireland, was built between 3100 and 2900 BCE and is aligned with the winter solstice.

- In 3000 BCE, Sumerian Cuneiform emerged from the proto-literate Uruk period, allowing the codification of beliefs and the creation of detailed historical religious records. The second phase of Stonehenge is completed and appears to function as the first enclosed cremation cemetery in the British Isles.

- 2635 to 2610 BCE, The oldest surviving Egyptian Pyramid is commissioned by the Pharaoh Djoser.

- In 2600 BCE, Stonehenge began to take on the form of its final phase, which we know today. The wooden posts were replaced with bluestone. It started to take on a more complex setup—including an altar, portal, station stones, etc.- and showed consideration of solar alignments.

- 2560 BCE, The approximate time that is accepted as the completion of the Great Pyramid of Giza, the oldest pyramid of the Giza Plateau.

- 2494 to 2345 BCE, The first of the oldest surviving religious texts, the Pyramid Texts, are composed in Ancient Egypt.

- 2200 BCE, the Minoan Civilization in Crete develops. Citizens worship various Goddesses.

Hang in there, my friends. Exploring the evolution of faith is essential when discussing religion.

- The earliest surviving versions of the Sumerian Epic of Gilgamesh (originally titled "He who Saw the Deep" (Sha Naqba īmuru) or "Surpassing All Other Kings" (Shūtur eli sharrī)) were written between 2150 and 2000 BCE.

• 2000 to 1850 BCE, The traditionally accepted period in which the Judeo-Christian/Islamic patriarchal figure Abraham lived. Likely born in Ur Kaśdim or Haran and died in Machpelah, Canaan.

• 1600 BCE, the ancient development of Stonehenge came to an end.

Keep in mind that all this is still 1,600 years before the birth of Jesus.

• 1351 or 1353 BCE, Reign of Akhenaten in Ancient Egypt. Akhenaten is sometimes credited with starting the earliest known monotheistic religion.

• 1250 BCE is the suggested time for the biblical Exodus of the Israelites from Egypt.

• 1200 to 600 BCE, The Upanishads (Vedic texts or Vedas - a large body of religious texts originating in ancient India.) are composed which contain the earliest emergence of some of the central religious concepts of Hinduism, Buddhism, and Jainism

• 1200 BCE, The Greek Dark Age begins.

• 1200 BCE, Olmecs built the earliest pyramids and temples in Central America.

• 950 BCE, The Torah, the core texts of Judaism and the foundation of later Abrahamic religions, is believed to be given by God to Moses

Keep in mind that 6,550 years have passed since we started this monotonous journey through time.

- 800 BCE, The Greek Dark Age ends.

- 563 BCE, Gautama Buddha, the founder of Buddhism, is born.

- 551 BCE, Confucius, founder of Confucianism, is born.

- 399 BCE, Socrates is tried for impiety (Godliness, sin).

- 150 BCE, The oldest surviving Hebrew Bible manuscripts date to about the 2nd century BCE (fragmentary).

- 100 BCE to 500 CE, The Yoga Sūtras of Patañjali constituting the foundational texts of Yoga are composed.

- 63 BCE, Pompey captured Jerusalem and annexed Judea as a Roman client kingdom.

If you're still awake - damn, I hope you aren't driving, we have reached the end of the timeline. I know it was a bit long, but it's important to look at this in the context of human evolution. To be true to attribution, this timeline came from Wikipedia.

There are other timelines on the Internet. If you are interested, I encourage you to explore all the information available. The Internet has put the complete knowledge of humanity and all the universities at our fingertips. Some accounts will vary one way or another, possibly motivated by ideology, but the fact is that we have been in the business of developing religious ceremonies for a very long time.

I feel a need at this point, no doubt prompted by a couple of glasses of good red wine, to apologize once again for that lengthy timeline. But it seems necessary to drive home the point about religious evolution. This shit didn't happen overnight.

It also seems important to note that all the aforementioned religious evolution occurred in the 3,000 years before Jesus was born; before Mohammed was born, and most of it before Buddha was around, which is believed to be between the 4th and 6th centuries BCE.

Now, I would like to direct you back to my comments describing how change is predictable. Hopefully, you recall the baking of a cake analogy: if you have a common set of circumstances occurring in different places, you will get a similar result in more than one place.

Look at the 3,000 years before Jesus and the 2,000 years since. It should be obvious that humans were ripe for a spiritual journey that previous belief systems had not fulfilled. Or perhaps they had, and the evolution of our minds and our knowledge of our world demanded new answers. In the recent past, devotion to religion seems to have waned. What might replace this? Time will tell.

Humans have been searching all over the world for answers to the questions of why we are here and what happens after we die.

To delve into the history of every religion and interrelationships since the beginning of time would require a dissertation of immense proportions that I suspect no one wants to endure, and would demand a great deal of study and research on my part. I'm too old and lazy for that. The odds of anyone staying with this rant to the end are minuscule at best as it is.

After the previous timeline, we find ourselves at the beginning of the Common Era (CE), once known as AD, a Christian-centric term. I believe the move to CE was a concession to the politically correct folks in the world of which I am one, but personally, with a considerably less virulent form of correctness than some people, at least most of the time.

Nevertheless, the old tags of BC and AD were based on the birth of Jesus, a decidedly Christian-centric reference. As such, they suggested to the rest of the world that their history didn't matter, that we didn't become a viable species on the planet until after the birth of Jesus, and that the advent of Jesus and the subsequent rise of Christianity based on the teachings of Jesus started the "real" calendar.

This had to have been seen as a significant slight at best and was not, I suspect, lost on the Jews, Hindus, and any number of Far Eastern religions that preceded Jesus by a thousand years or more, not to mention the ones that came later. Why not BM – before Mohammed, and AM – after Mohammed, or BB – before Buddha, and so on? So, in the name of fairness, Before the Common Era (BCE) and the Common Era (CE) do seem more appropriate, not to mention more respectful and inclusive, although even the term "common" seems dismissive.

Permit me to characterize the Middle East as the Western World, as opposed to the Far East, and in the interest of simplicity, I am suggesting the Middle East is the Where of modern Western religion. The Ancient Egyptians, a term generically applied to a number of societies of the time, including the Babylonians, codified religion at the time.

It is apparent from research that there was a belief in gods, but they were still a mysterious entity. At some point, and we find evidence of this well before Egypt and Ancient Greece, various leaders like Pharaohs and Emperors began to define themselves as descendants of the gods.

This did a couple of things for what must have been a group of highly egotistical people, not all that unusual within the ranks of royalty. It gave more gravitas to their pronouncements from the throne, elevated them to a status that was revered, and suggested a degree of infallibility.

The idea of a leader who was related to the gods initially sat well with the masses because it put a human face on these mysterious and invisible gods and gave them the sense that they had a direct conduit to the gods they could see, if not touch, their pharaohs and emperors. As a bonus, it also discouraged any pretenders to the throne from engaging in palace intrigue, lest they invite the wrath of the gods by messing with one of their relatives.

Over time, as these emperors and pharaohs misbehaved, married their sisters, or committed various sex acts with their mothers, brothers, sisters, and, unfortunately, even their children, the most common and uneducated among the masses began to question the piety of these self-declared gods. Much like politicians who promise the moon and leaders of churches who profess all manner of values as they misbehave, then crash and burn, there is no doubt that they are nothing more than the rest of us — humans.

While Akhenaten of Egypt, remember, it appears that he may have been one of the first to suggest a single god and is thought to possibly have been the first to promote a monotheistic religion, i.e., a single deity, the idea didn't catch on all that well for another thousand years or so.

The Torah is thought to have been given to Moses by God about 400 years after Akhenaten did his single God thing. Coincidence? I think not. The people of the time must have known what old Akhenaten had been talking about based on the stories passed down over generations and conversations at dinner and at happy hour, and some people must have embraced the concept.

There had to have been a great deal of discussion and debate in the public gathering places over a led-lined chalice of mind-expanding wine about the theory of a single god versus the many gods that had dominated human thought for thousands of years.

If you think about it, a single god simplifies life as opposed to keeping track of and trying to appease multiple gods. When a calamity occurred, who did we need to appease? Which God just rained fire and brimstone down on the tribe? It must have been perplexing and brought about the unnecessary sacrifice of many... we can only hope, animals.

There was likely disagreement over which God had caused the ruckus. Those who had their favorite God might have defended him or her, although it was most likely a 'him.' The single-god approach, a much simpler concept, made life a lot easier. As we know today, based on the audience of FOX News, humans have a predilection for simple answers, whether factual or not.

It seems likely that many people, over many years and probably millennia, believed there may have been only one God. As you can see by conducting a little research on the topic of religion, there is a liberal sprinkling of terms such as "it is thought" or "may have" throughout religious texts as opposed to "it is a fact."

Such statements tend to muddy the historical waters. With a shortage of documentation beyond the writings of the flat earth society over a thousand years ago, there needs to be more proof to support the many theories that abound.

One also presumes that voicing the idea of this single, almighty God in a society that proclaimed the top banana as being related to one or the other of the all-powerful gods that were fashionable at the time could get you jammed up big time with the emperor or a pharaoh. This kind of discussion took place in private and out of earshot of any authorities, waiting for society to evolve to the point where most people were ready for a new idea.

Back to our misbehaving Emperors for a moment. Their followers began to seriously doubt that these people were, in fact, gods and began the process of dethroning these impostors. Interestingly, this included knocking the noses off their statues, a profuse practice at the time that I still find confusing.

These rebels against the established religion of the day were unknowingly creating a spiritual vacuum. My research, limited by my lack of persistence accompanied by a degree of complacency, failed to uncover where this tradition of de-nosing those who fell from favor originated.

We all know by now that nature abhors a vacuum, and that man's mind is both creative and devious. Somewhere along the line, due in part to people's disillusionment with the status quo, the drunken, incestuous, pedophilia behavior—choose your favorite adjective—of those who were calling the shots from their golden thrones caused the believers to change their allegiance and gravitate toward a new belief system.

The one God theory, an all-powerful entity securely stashed away in something called heaven and well away from the temptations of mortal humans, must have had a strong appeal. He was offered up as infallible, and with the notion that He created us in His image, what was not to like?

Before I lose some readers with my sarcasm, let me hasten to add that while I believe a significant number of religious leaders are motivated by something other than a true calling to God, some do feel they are called.

I question the greedy ones whose motives I question. They have been enchanted by the promise of power, adulation, and perhaps riches and lack any earnest desire to lead the masses from darkness into the light.

They are more likely to lead their flock to the ATM and encourage them to empty their accounts in the name of the church.

I also believe that many, and perhaps even most of the devout throughout history, were and are today sincere in their beliefs and teachings. They genuinely want to make the world a better place by preaching what they are sure is what God intended for us all, at least as they interpret His intentions. I am obviously excluding any of those who preach intolerance and hatred from their pulpits.

Unfortunately, like corporate leaders who start off with the best of intentions, religious leaders have two fundamental problems. A message that promises Hell and damnation if you wander from the path will not make many people sign up. That is different from the sort of Labor Day mattress sales message that is going to bring crowds to your place of worship. It's toe the line, and I hope you are accepted into heaven.

The second problem, and one that I'm sure each of them swore would never happen to them, in the same way that politicians and corporate CEOs believe they are above all that sort of political pressure and tomfoolery, is the siren temptress of power and greed and the temptation of the human body. They begin to convince themselves that they have the answers, and a kind of royal myopia prevents them from seeing much of anything else.

The assumption that everyone thinks as they do and will be blind to their missteps has been the downfall of many leaders, religious and political. This very human failure will not end any time soon, as we are all susceptible to flattery, whether exterior or self-inflicted.

We find in the many teachings about God that, at times, he is a benevolent God and, at times, a very vengeful God. This should seem an oxymoron to many people, myself included, and so it must have seemed even to those of ancient times. This leads us to my next topic, the Devil.

From my readings, I learned that a number of civilizations suspected a dark character existed who, like the gods, no one could see. This character from the underworld was responsible for, well, drunkenness and almost everything from petty thievery to mass murder, acting stupid, coveting their neighbor's house and possessions, and banging another person's spouse. It would seem that Lucifer was responsible for all manner of deviant behavior that a given society deemed to be against the accepted rules at any particular time in history.

The advent of the Devil is yet another development that makes a lot of sense. Because the majority of people are sincere in any endeavor, they are bewildered that they would allow themselves to wander from the path they have chosen to follow, as are those close to them who know them to be pious and honest people.

If we are that weak as a species despite being zealous adherents to our religion, there must be another answer: we can't be simply that flawed and without redemption; after all, didn't God create us just like him? It's the work of the Devil that causes us to go astray, not any innate moral turpitude. Problem solved. We blame the Devil and throw ourselves on the mercy (the merciful side) of an angry God.

Christianity has developed quite an obsession with our red-faced, horned, and cloven-hoofed friend from the center of the earth. With the advent of Christianity and the writing of the Bible's New Testament, we are inundated with references to the Devil and all of his negative influences on the common man and woman.

Seriously, is even the Devil a man? According to Christianity, Eve in the Garden was the bad guy, née woman. Was she the first Devil, or was it the fallen angel Lucifer in the form of a snake who was said to become the Devil around at the time of the Garden? As I write this, I'm not sure whether to capitalize the Devil or not.

Let's digress for a moment back to the time of multiple gods. There were good gods and evil gods. Gods who rained the wonderful events of life on humans, and the gods who apparently experienced a great deal of joy in screwing with humans and making their lives miserable.

You had a choice of gods. You could pick your favorite gods and put their images all around your cave, hut, or whatever you called home. You could wear them around your neck or tattoo them on your body; you could even eat and drink foods purported to be part of their bodies. I don't think Christianity, specifically the Catholics, invented that idea. There was no end of the ways to honor the deity of your choice.

The bad gods? You could burn them in effigy, toss images of them into the latrine, or whatever served as an outhouse those centuries ago. The origin of the Evil Eye can be traced back to Mesopotamia, one of the earliest human civilizations. It was believed that certain individuals could cast curses through their eyes; often, women were to blame (no surprise there!)

The Greeks picked up on this and had what was known as "Baskania". The Greek Orthodox Church has recognized the kako mati since the establishment of the faith. The church calls it Vaskania (pronounced Vas-ka-nee-a) and has a special prayer made especially to help cure those who have fallen under the curse.

Romans also adopted the belief in the Evil Eye, referring to it as "invidia" or "ocular malevolence." In Turkey, it is known as the "nazar" or "nazar boncugu." In Spain and Latin America, it is called the "mal de ojo." In Arabic-speaking countries, it is referred to as "ayn al-hasud."

The belief in the battle between good and evil has persisted for millennia.

The one-God theory messed up how people worshiped. Only one God? Was he or she responsible for everything, both the good and bad? How could that be? How could this God, who many believe created us in his image (tall, skinny, male, female, fat, black, brown, white — he must be a most amusing visage if he is all these things), treat us so cruelly at times? He must love us to have risen us from the dust of his image.

It must have been challenging to get people to accept the Reader's Digest version of a single god after living with such various deities from which to choose. A little reading of the history of the New World and the challenges faced by the predominantly Catholic missionaries in convincing, or rather forcing, the indigenous people of the New World to change gods bears that out.

I have no doubt these questions were raised in the early days of monotheistic religious practices. Religious leaders needed to persuade the masses to embrace their new teachings. They had to put some distance between this new God and the pagan gods that these folks were reluctant to divorce.

This must have created a challenge for the leaders of the one-god approach to religion. Some people must have been curious and skeptical, as we humans universally are when confronted with change.

Others may have been educated, and some may have been inherently more intellectual on a practical level. Whatever their circumstance, many people questioned everything in life, including the existing religious dogma.

Of course, there were the sheep who needed to be herded in the right direction—there always were. Like the pack animals we are, there are those who lead and those who follow, comfortable letting the leaders make the decisions.

Throughout history, most religions have used the sheep, those willing to follow unquestioningly en masse, to squelch the intellectuals by bleating in the streets and in every public venue, often carrying torches and pitchforks, decrying that those who questioned the teachings of the church, i.e., God, were evil, and possibly possessed by the Devil.

These unbelievers had to be ferreted out and either converted to believers or face extinction. This formula of demonizing your adversaries has a lengthy and proven track record of success. We have only to look at the murderous and radical factions within Islam to see that process still at work today, but Judaism and Christianity are both stained with the same intolerance and bigotry, so no one gets a pass.

Back to our ruddy and oven-tanned friend, the Devil. In fiction, the basis of any good story is the protagonist, or the good guy, and the antagonist, the bad guy. Conflict is the backbone of any successful novel or movie. And the only acceptable outcome in the minds of most people is for the good guy to dispatch the bad guy.

Now that the leaders had dispensed with all the "bad" gods, who used to get the blame for the bad stuff that happened to folks, who do we vilify now? Voilà, the Devil! "The Devil made me do it."

You might remember that line made famous by Flip Wilson on The Flip Wilson Show. If you're too young to remember who this is, Google him, and you can check out some videos; he was a pretty funny guy for his time.

Now we had a foil for our new and benevolent God, someone to blame for all of humankind's dalliances and aberrant behavior that a benevolent god would never have visited on his chosen people.

Early leaders of just about any religion must have recognized that self-governance was not a strong suit of the typical human. With no laws nor agencies to enforce them and no religious teachings with the threat of severe punishment for our misdeeds, we showed a certain fondness for behaving like, well, animals.

Of course, we are animals and not as far removed from our chimpanzee cousins as we might like to think. Nevertheless, a perfect God couldn't possibly have created flawed humans if we were created in his image; there had to be another explanation. Therefore, the Devil must be perverting God's perfect design. There's nothing more satisfying than a fall guy or scapegoat.

It is nothing more than critical thinking at work. If A and B could be proven to be a fact - but wait, there was no way of proving any of this. Nevertheless, we will claim that the theory of God, heaven, the Devil, et al is irrefutable, which is not possible.

The Devil, the fallen angel, if we are to accept the scriptures and the burning fires of Hell, and an eternity of shoveling hot coals or feces, or something at least as distasteful, was meant to be a significant deterrent to most of the frightened early humans still trying to shake the bonds of suspicion and belief in goblins, witches.

The Devil provided another benefit, one the Catholics have used as well as anyone. If the Devil made you do it, then you can't be solely to blame for coloring outside the lines. In fact, you might even have been possessed by the Devil. Thus, there are marvelous Catholic rituals such as confession and exorcism.

None of this happened overnight, nor did the masses throw aside their various idols because someone who claimed to have the inside track on religion told them to do so. The truth is that it took a very long time and a lot of persuasion to get the people to embrace these new ideas, which is the essence of social evolution.

Take the Catholic Church as a prime example. To win over their flock, in addition to threats of damnation, the church managed to blend many of the pagan holidays into the practice of Catholicism. They really had no choice because the populace stubbornly refused to give up their favorite festivals and idols.

Christmas, the celebration of the birth of Jesus, Easter, and Valentine's Day all have either pagan beginnings or involve, in some instances, celebratory trappings left over from pagan rituals. This pronouncement can make devout Christians foam at the mouth, but it is accurate and yet another example of religilution.

The Catholic Church, sort of the grandaddy of Christianity, at least in any organized fashion, claims to have started with the birth of Jesus. They believe their church was established by the disciple Paul. And by connecting plenty of questionable dots, they stand by that claim.

Christianity was busy trying to convert pagans from their worship of a passel of gods and various pagan rituals based on magical and mystical events to a single god. The fact that Christianity was also unproven and primarily dealt with mysticism helped the conversion of the masses.

The pagans knew how to party, and their festivals, often involving a bit of drink and inappropriate behavior, proved to be a bigger draw than the solemn, austere teachings of early Christians.

The early days of Christianity or Catholicism were relatively chaotic, with a number of principles cited as perhaps the first Pope. The Catholic Church considers Peter, one of Jesus' disciples, the first Pope, but that is fairly subjective.

There is St. Linus around the year 64, St. Anacletus, St. Evaristus in 97, and the list goes on. An argument can be made that Emperor Constantine may deserve the label since he legitimized Christianity during his reign from 306 to 337 CE.

The bottom line is that divine intervention wasn't at play here; politics, power, and influence in the right places brought Christianity to the forefront as one of the world's major religions.

Religions, in general, were the construct of individuals, most often men, who found fault with the way society conducted itself. They sought a way to reign in the masses, to get them to conform to some behavior pattern they deemed acceptable.

Those elements and general dissatisfaction with the status quo provided the perfect recipe for change. In other words, like the predictability of a chocolate cake, the time was right, and the people seized the opportunity to throw off the bonds of the old beliefs and follow the piper down the road.

So now we have the recipe for religion, pretty much as we know it today. The good guy, God, and the bad guy, the Devil, and a plethora of religious leaders and zealots over a couple of thousand years only too willing to help us follow the path to truth and salvation as they visualized that path, even if that meant discrimination against those who disagreed, and worse, the destruction of any nonbelievers.

I won't go on about that last statement. There is ample evidence of acts perpetrated in the name of God during the Crusades and Inquisitions, and today. This information is readily available if you do a little research and read any number of terrific books that give a historical account of such events. Be prepared to be horrified if you delve into this topic.

Yet, we dare to call radical Muslims terrorists, which, of course, some are. But they are far from the first religious zealots to use fear and terror to try to get their way.

Time for another caveat. I draw no distinction between radical Muslims and radical Christians, radical Jews, or any other extreme religious point of view that sees their mission as the subjugation of others to their way of thinking through whatever means necessary, including killing.

A good deal of this scenario played out in the first 1,500 years of the modern religion era, first in the Middle East, and then as it spread, or was spread by invading armies, throughout Europe.

The Jews popularized the one-God theory and were, to a large degree, the only game in town for a long time. They had their detractors in those early millennia, a couple of thousand years before Christ. Still, they persevered; if they didn't always thrive, they survived.

Summarizing the where of religion? It's all over the damn place throughout documented history and likely for millennia before that. It perfectly demonstrates the notion of religious evolution as well as or better than any of the other W's.

How?

How could this all happen? How can it be that religion has a hold on modern humans the way it did on our ancestors, who lacked the scientific and life knowledge that we have today?

That question may never be answered. How do people choose a lover? How do we decide what food we like, what color of clothing is our favorite, or what kind of car we want?

I'm going out on a limb here, but there are several reasons for how we make these and other choices. We inherit some tendencies from our parents and past generations. That might be controversial in some circles, but I happen to think it is true.

It seems probable that the strongest influence will come from our nearest ancestors, our parents. But I also believe there are latent tendencies that may not have been manifested in our parents, tendencies that came from their parents, the generation closest to them, or even further back, and can pop out in future generations.

Our parents may not have had a musical bone in their bodies, but suddenly, one of their children becomes a musical prodigy. If you could dig deep enough, you would likely find a more distant relative with those talents.

I also believe in a giant roulette wheel, the wheel of personality traits. While genetics will play a significant role in who we are and what we like and dislike, we all have just about every kind of gene in our body that can possibly be hosted by a human. When that egg and sperm go into the big Mixmaster, almost anything can happen.

An example. Your parents both have blue eyes, and you have brown eyes. No one in the family in anyone's memory had brown eyes, but there you are. The jokes about your father being the mailman or the gas meter reader aside, it could have been that a long ago, a relative had brown eyes. That gene laid dormant in the family until it came to life in you. We carry all the genes for every color of eye known, and that little steel ball can fall in any slot on the wheel at any time.

Staying with the roulette wheel analogy, if your family has a tendency toward blue eyes, the majority of slots on the wheel will be blue or variations of blue, but there will also be brown and green eye genes, and while the odds favor blue eyes, the others can manifest.

I wrote a paper years ago in a psychology class where I tried to explain this concept. We studied the greats of psychology, Jung, Freud, and Adler, as well as others. We studied theories that suggested everything from as few as six personality types to over 4,000.

At some point, I decided it was futile to nail down the exact number; even that may vary with each individual. There are, however, a few traits that can be generalized across the human species. Current thinking lumps them into five major categories: openness, conscientiousness, extraversion, agreeableness, and neuroticism.

Being a visual person, I developed a sketch for my thesis of how I saw traits playing out.

I'll try to explain it. Visualize a stack of panels, perhaps plastic, so you can see down through the stack. Each panel is about a half-inch thick, so we can write on the edges of the panel. Around the edges of each of these panels are the titles of competing personality traits like happy or angry, quiet or noisy. For instance, on the top panel, we might have introvert written on one edge and extrovert written on the adjoining edge. On the face of this panel are two crossing lines that intersect in the center. Each line has a scale from minus ten on one end to plus ten on the other end. Where the lines intersect in the middle of the panel is the zero point for each of the lines. Now, you can create a stack of these panels with varying and competing personality traits.

Genetics puts you somewhere on each of these panels when you're born. You might be right on the zero on one panel and hard over to plus ten on another panel of traits - it's all dictated by genetics and chance, or what I like to think of as the genetic roulette wheel. Whether you are in the center or on the extreme of specific traits, you now enter life and begin to have experiences, both good and bad, that can nudge your tendencies in one direction or the other.

The more centered you are, the more changeable you are likely to be. If you are hard over to the extreme of specific traits, life events will be more difficult to move you on the scale.

This theory tries to portray the idea that regardless of the number and type of competing personality traits humans may have, we all have a starting place based on what we are born with, our inheritance, so to speak, plus that crazy roulette wheel sometimes dropping you randomly on the chart. But for the most part, this is what "nature" gave you at the beginning of life.

Now, let's talk about nurture. All the things we are exposed to, parenting, either good or bad, outside influences, be that peers in school, video games if you believe those change personalities, or significant emotional events such as a near-death experience, and a myriad of other factors that affect our lives as we are maturing start to move us on the charts.

All of these experiences and more will begin to nudge your personality proclivities on the graph in one direction or another. How much of an effect nurture can have depends on the starting point and your perception of the events that are trying to move you about on the chart.

Looking at the top layer, we'll assume it is labeled happy and sad. If you start out at or near the intersection of the two lines, that would be considered a neutral position and presumably the easiest to influence in my theory. If, on the other hand, you are at the extreme end of plus/minus 10 on one of the personality graphs, it should be much harder to move you toward the center.

Now, imagine that you are looking down through all the panels, whether ten or a hundred. There is a collection of starting points on each panel, and all those points for your collective personality. Suppose you're seen by others to be a happy and positive person. In that case, the dots on each of the panels will favor the happy and positive side of the spectrum of the traits.

In addition to bragging that I received an A-minus, my point in discussing this paper is to demonstrate my contention that you begin life with a kind of built-in program that is the starting point for your personality. Just how rigid that program is and how receptive you are to change will depend on what you inherited from your ancestors and the luck of the old genetic roulette wheel.

One more quick example of how and why personalities can be hardwired would be to look at physical characteristics. As a man - I'm not qualified to speak for women - and you inherit the genetics of a jockey, i.e., you are 4 feet 10 inches tall and weigh 100 pounds, soaking wet. You can spend eight hours a day in the gym forever, but you will never be 6 feet 2 inches tall and 195 pounds, rippling with the muscles of a competitive bodybuilder. You can undoubtedly change your physique, but only within the bounds of what the roulette wheel gave you to begin with. The same holds true for the ladies, but I am not dumb enough to start describing the physical characteristics of females.

Our emotional makeup, whether we are angry or happy, whether we are inclined to depression, and our sexual orientation or preference are all determined at birth. If you are a hard-core heterosexual, no amount of nurture will make you gay, or vice versa. If you are in the center of the spectrum, you may want to explore bisexuality.

How does all this relate to the discussion of religious evolution? Some people are more psychologically susceptible to suggestion and fear than others. To my way of thinking, that could make them amenable to wanting to believe in the mysteries offered by most religions. It seems to me that people who are innately fearful are more likely to believe in ghosts and embrace other supernatural theories and stories.

Depending on how virulent and militant the religious message is that individuals are receiving in whichever faith they choose to follow and where they began their journey on the personality trait scales, they may have the potential to tip all the way over to being religious zealots, and in extreme cases, violent fundamentalists like we have seen pop up in most major religions.

Still, this may not completely explain how or why we as a species seem to be vulnerable to believing in Santa Claus when we are children and all sorts of epic adventures as adults. This, too, is traceable to evolution.

Let's take one last trip back in time in our time machine. We'll stay with 50,000 years ago, although the answers may be further back than that. The oldest modern human remains found to date go back some 200,000 years. The earliest evidence of our bipedal human ancestors is four million years old, so we've been developing our brains for a long time.

Okay, so let's crank the machine to the maximum and go back four million years. If we are having fun guessing how people lived 50,000 years ago, we can have a blast with the folks from four million years ago.

One has to presume, or at least I do, that when our evolutionary line first stood on their back legs, their mental capacity was below the family pet's. After all, the family pet is also the product of evolution.

We began domesticating dogs some 12,000 years ago. If you use twelve years as the average lifespan of a dog, that would be 1,000 generations of dogs learning how to live with and pushing the emotional buttons of us humans. They have done a damn good job of figuring us out. Is it any wonder we walk down the street with a plastic bag picking up their poop?

Back to our first bipedal ancestors. Their brains could not have been much more advanced than what we now refer to as our reptilian brain, or Triune Brain, that brain stem with a wee knob on the top that is surrounded by the new brain we evolved over the millennia. In the interest of fairness, and balanced bullshit, let me say that it is a theory; it is certainly controversial, but one I find totally coherent. While we may have had bursts of brain development over time, we started with very little.

Suppose we started out with a brain that functioned on a level only slightly higher than an earthworm; probably an exaggeration. In that case, everything could most likely scare the crap out of us. An explanation, any explanation for events that were far beyond our comprehension, was quickly absorbed as fact. It was the only thing that would let us sleep at night.

Now, I have to ask you for a leap of faith one more time, but if you have stuck with me to this point, you have become accustomed to that request. If we did start out as quivering masses of flesh paralyzed with fear and susceptible to just about any story that soothed our paranoia, and we continued to intake all these myths for a significant part of four million years. In that case, our brains should be seriously hardwired to accept unprovable legends. In other words, we love fairy tales, and religious texts are full of them.

As children, we readily accept the myths of Santa, the Easter Bunny, goblins, witches, and ghosts. In history, numerous adults have long accepted these fairy tales as fact, at least in terms of witches, warlocks, and the like.

Another observation I have made that tends to support this theory is that we love to have the bejesus scared out of us. Why else would we flock to movies where people are butchered with chainsaws, ripped to pieces by horrible monsters with long fingernails, or eaten alive by zombies? Something in our nature (our evolution) or maybe that old brain wants to believe in the supernatural and things like little green people from outer space.

How does all this relate to understanding how we can buy into stories about someone we can't see, have never met, and events that took place 2,000 years ago but never seem to happen now? Is it that old brain, the reptilian brain, that thrives on this kind of story to survive?

Is it that ancient part of our brains that governs things like breathing, swallowing, pooping, etc? We don't have to think about those bodily functions; we do them automatically. Fight or flight wells up from deep in that brain.

We can learn breathing techniques in yoga class, but when we go to sleep at night, we don't have to think about breathing. Our bodies function just the same thanks to that part of our brain that keeps us alive, sometimes despite our best efforts. Our heart beats, and our liver and kidneys do their work, all automatically, and have been doing so since before we stood on our hind legs. In many ways, we are on automatic pilot.

If the origins of our fears, fears that require us to believe that scary things are out there, are lodged in that old brain and have been at work for millions of years, it will not easily be undone.

Take the instinct for fight or flight as an example. Now that we live in a very different world than our ancient ancestors, the intellectual capacity in our brain can override instinct. However, the instinct will still surface in the right situation, like those bad dudes in a dark alley that wanted a piece of your ass. When we get close enough to realize they are Mormon missionaries taking a weed break, then we can corral that instinct and quiet it down because we recognize this was a false signal from our brain.

Perhaps, thousands of years in the future, as our world becomes less and less fearful, the old brain will lose that fear function. Take our appendix, for example; no one knows what function it served, and it has become extinct. Our brain may lose functions that are no longer needed. That assumes the brain is capable of evolving, and I wonder whether that is true or not; it appears to have mostly stayed the same for a very long time. We can stuff more knowledge in there, but we have a hard time shaking some of the old instincts.

For now, in varying degrees, we continue needing to feed that part of the brain that wants to be frightened because it operates on the presumption it has to protect us from our fears. Think of that as a practice session for the real thing, but the real thing is no longer real.

And since so much of what religion relies on is fear, we will not soon see religion fade into the past to join such behaviors as human sacrifice, burning of witches, etc.

There you have my how for why religion has been able to grab us by the short hairs and keep a hold on us despite all the knowledge we have gained over the last 2,000 years.

We are a little like our pet dogs and cats. I am convinced that they have learned a great deal more than they knew when they partnered with humans 12,000 years ago, yet they remain dogs, doing all the things that dogs do.

We're in the home stretch, just a bit more to read

How?

Man, I bet you thought this was never coming. Congratulations on hanging in there. "You're a better man than I am, Gunga Din!"

It strikes me that it may be time to summarize this stream of consciousness or what some may see as nonsense, but I hope most will think of it as an attempt to understand the human mind and our path down the evolutionary road of religion.

As I tried to say at the beginning of all this, I am not anti-religion. True, I am not a believer, and it may seem that I am suggesting that those who are might be either conditioned, jejune, or neurotic, but I honestly am not. I get why many people need religion in their lives, even as I am nonplussed by the fanaticism of some of those willing to kill and die to try to change my mind.

Am I baffled that so many people cling to these ancient beliefs in the light of all we've learned since the times when we believed there was a thunder god and the world was flat? Of course, I am, but that doesn't mean that I am trying to degrade or in any way demote these people; I simply don't understand how and why they cling to these ancient myths. But then, I don't understand why some people would drink light beer - we are all different, and that makes us unique.

Like it or not, we are a product of our history, genetics, evolution, and all that entails. In some ways, most of us are helpless to deny who we are.

Am I some enlightened philosopher, idiot savant, or simply delusional? I have no idea. You be the judge. I am the product of the same genetic roulette wheel and nurturing forces that acted on my personality as a child, just like each of you and the people I have talked about in this book. No more and no less.

I will remain amazed until the day I die that people in the 21st century continue to hold on to the beliefs from the Dark Ages, and even further back than that, for all the reasons I have set forth earlier.

Yet, as I stated earlier, if you want to dance naked around a boulder in the moonlight, go for it; just don't ask me to join in the festivities.

I am basically a product of the 1950s and '60s generations that proclaimed, "Live and let live." Really. I have no right or divine direction from any higher power to tell you how to live your life, nor do you have the right or similar direction to tell me how to live mine.

As the Buddhists say, basically, do no harm. That is a philosophy I wish the entire world could embrace. With that, I will sign off and wish you the happiest life that anyone could imagine. Be peaceful and loving, and when you are lying on your deathbed, have as few regrets as humanly possible.

The word peace exists in every language on the planet. Muslims typically greet each other by saying, 'As-salamu alaykum,' which translates to 'Peace be upon you.' "Peace, my friend" in Spanish is paz mi amigo. In Italian, they say pach-e amico mio. In French, Paix mon ami. In German, Frieden, mein Freund. In Swedish, Fred min vän, and in Irish, it is síocháin mo chara (pronounced something like see-o-han moh Hara). Gaelic is a tricky language to speak.

It doesn't matter which language you speak; it's what is in your heart. Imagine a world where the first thought that came to everyone's mind and the first words out of their mouths when meeting or dealing with anyone from any part of the world, a different nationality, race, sex, or religion, was "Peace."

Epilogue

I have now produced an eBook and audiobook for this essay, and that process has been a labor of love, a journey, and learning a number of new skills. Whether others will find any of this of interest remains to be seen. If I were to realize tonight that this was my last day on earth, I would feel that perhaps I have left something of value to the world.

That something - is a discussion that will hopefully stimulate people's thinking. We have this marvelous organ inside our cranium, and it deserves to do more than watch the NFL (which I love, by the way) or some innocuous show like The Bachelor. Peace and love, my friends.

Again, I thank my wife, Gale, for her love and patience, my wonderful children, Tracy, Joey, and Sean, and all my friends who have endured me climbing onto one of my soapboxes over the years. Your willingness to let me use you as a sounding board has contributed to my understanding of life.

With that, I bid you adieu. Thank you for reading my book.

End Credits

Thank you again for reading From Coconut Trees To Cult by me, Mike Davis. I truly hope you enjoyed it. It has been a labor of love for me, a love for writing, and a passion for the book's topic.

While producing both this eBook and the audiobook, I learned quite a few new skills. First, you have to write differently for an audience that will be listening rather than reading print on the page. Then, there are the protocols for recording, editing, and assembling the book. While I made a few false starts, I have to credit a number of applications I used to complete the task.

First, I'm an Apple guy and used Pages to do the first draft. Then, after casting about for a bit, I settled on a site for the audio version, ElevenLabs, elevenlabs.io, to create my cloned voice and find a suitable voice to use for narration. For this eBook, I relied on Pages and will publish it on Draft2digital. Both sites and their methodology were, for me, quite intuitive.

I used Audacity to prepare my audio files. I found a site, alexexum.com, that directed me to use Audacity to make my files ACX-compliant. And. Finally, after researching and reading ways to get my book in front of listeners, I chose to work with the good folks at my find away voices.com

I look forward to my next audio and eBook, Almost An Orphan, which tells my personal story, my autobiography, if you will, which some folks have found interesting.

Don't miss out!

Visit the website below and you can sign up to receive emails whenever Mike Davis publishes a new book. There's no charge and no obligation.

https://books2read.com/r/B-A-ARUGB-LCQOE

BOOKS 2 READ

Connecting independent readers to independent writers.

About the Author

I have spent most of my life exploring why we humans do and think what we do. I have reached a few conclusions, but my life has been a continuous learning curve, and as such, I hope to learn something new every day. I write about my thoughts, conclusions, and ideas with the hope that it might help others see a different perspective.

I speculate on topics from Artificial Intelligence to zoology. My thoughts and opinions are often wrapped in humor, but are always meant to broaden our understanding of who we are.

Read more at https://www.irishmikedavis.com.

www.ingramcontent.com/pod-product-compliance
Lightning Source LLC
Chambersburg PA
CBHW021952170726
47994CB00020B/232